Jonathan Lighter

"The Best Antiwar Song Ever Written"

The country gave much to those who came—and it received from them as well. Now, sometimes the gifts were grudgingly given, from one to another, and sometimes they were freely given—lovingly given. The people brought an ideal of freedom: the land gave them ground to let that freedom grow. At times the people forgot—as all men can forget—the very freedom they'd come to nurture and share. But fortunately—we've never forgotten all at once. Enough of us were around at any given time to remember, and to fight if necessary. Freedom is something that we owe this nation for what it has given us. We've even killed each other for the sake of that debt. And men in other lands have killed and died for the sake of freedom. We've taken their heritage to ourselves—as we've taken their songs.

Tommy Makem then took the stage with the Clancy Bros. and introduced their rendition—alternately fiery and tender and with the choral refrains in military tempo—by observing that:

> One of the most popular songs of the time of the American Civil War was a song called "When Johnny Comes Marching Home Again." That song had an ancestor in Ireland—much as the notion of freedom and the idea of fighting and dying for it had an ancestor in every part of the world. This song is called "Johnny, I Hardly Knew Ye."[3]

When Makem and the Clancys left the stage, Preston told the audience hyperbolically that "a million men did not come home from the Civil War." In Luxon's later performance, his histrionic anger, which builds from an incipit of seemingly wistful recollection, eventually explodes in crescendo at the line about the eyeless egg. Versions like his forgo a key Makem-Clancy element: the implied defiance of the enemy and ultimate moral victory for the mangled soldier detectable in the way they always varied the last chorus: *The enemy never slew ye!* It is the only line in the song that might sustain Preston's emphasis on fighting for freedom regardless of the cost, a punch line that makes the song a monument to the spirit of a fighting patriot. It is also a line that was original with the group, though repeated by few other singers, presumably because the lyrics are too astonishing and horrible to support any interpretation but one: that of overwhelming personal tragedy, as in Benjamin Luxon's anguished performance.[4]

That "Johnny, I Hardly Knew Ye" is an anonymous song of Irish origin, created as a bitter indictment of war and long predating the War between the States, has become nearly universally accepted—endorsed by recording artists and by Alan Lomax, by the *Times* of London and the U.S. Library of Congress, and, through them, by the many amateur folksingers who perform it.[5] It is frequently said in such accounts that Union army bandmaster Patrick S. Gilmore's related composition, "When Johnny Comes Marching Home" (1863), with its idealized welcome for the representative soldier "Johnny," was an insidious rewrite that, in the words of historian Robert V. Wells, "clearly served the need for Civil War propaganda."[6] Gilmore's use of the Irish song's melody, stanzaic form, and situation is seen as a successfully manipulative effort to replace an earlier, more genuine work of art whose deeply pacifist message the war-makers could not allow to go unchallenged. Certainly the theme of Gilmore's lyrics, published under the *nom de plume* of "Louis Lambert" not long after the battle of Gettysburg and its staggering total of 46,000 casualties, bears an undeniable, albeit inverted, resemblance to that of the Irish song:

> When Johnny comes marching home again,
> Hurrah, hurrah!
> We'll give him a hearty welcome then,
> Hurrah, hurrah!
> The men will cheer, the boys will shout,
> The ladies, they will all turn out,
> And we'll all feel gay,
> When Johnny comes marching home.
>
> *[similarly]*
>
> The old church bell will peal with joy,...
> To welcome home our darling boy,...

The village lads and lassies say,
With roses they will strew the way…

Get ready for the Jubilee,…
We'll give the hero three times three…
The laurel wreath is ready now,
To place upon his loyal brow,….

Let love and friendship on that day,…
Their choicest treasures then display,…
And let each one perform some part,
To fill with joy the warrior's heart,
And we'll all feel gay,
When Johnny comes marching home. [7]

The prominent religious scholar and mythologist Wendy Doniger finds the transformation of the "Irish antiwar folksong, 'Johnny I Hardly Knew Ye,' into the pro-war American Civil War song, 'When Johnny Comes Marching Home'" nothing short of "amazing."[8] Surely such a thoroughgoing revision could not have been innocently created.

The closest reading to date of the text of "Johnny, I Hardly Knew Ye" is by Wells (2009), in a book on traditional song published by Cambridge University Press (2009). Wells, too, places the song in the context of the Civil War, and he carefully considers a frequently recorded final stanza—not performed on television by the Clancy Brothers or Bernard Luxon—that makes the song's pacifist sentiments crystal clear:

They're rolling out the guns again, Hurroo, hurroo!
They're rolling out the guns again, Hurroo, hurroo!
They're rolling out the guns again,
But they'll never take our sons again,
They'll never take our sons again!
Johnny, I'm swearin' to ye!

For a younger generation raised on video war games and having only a dim awareness of combat in Iraq and Afghanistan, much less the Civil War,

Wells states the obvious—that, unlike Gilmore's robust returning Johnny, "many soldiers did not come back, and many who did were unable to march." After relating that "so common were injuries during this war that a whole industry making prosthetic limbs developed after the conflict," Wells zeroes in on the lyrics:

> The Irish version, sometimes known as 'Drums and Guns,' is sung from the perspective of a woman welcoming home the wreck of her husband.... The recurring motif in the last line of the chorus grieves, 'Johnny I hardly knew you,' a cry that is equally powerful whether it refers to her trouble recognizing him or her regret that they had too little time together before he went to war. Faced with the fact that 'they're rolling out the guns again,' this wife and mother promises, 'They'll never take our sons again.' ...Few songs are so direct about the likely outcomes of wars for the soldiers and their families, while the blame is shared between Johnny, who was attracted to his 'guns and drums,' and the powerful 'they,' who are rolling out the guns again to feed the children of the poor to the dogs of war.[9]

This characterization rests uncomfortably both with Makem's perspective and with the general belief in the North that the preservation of the Union and the abolition of slavery were causes worth fighting for, a belief shared, for example, by both Abraham Lincoln and Karl Marx. The Civil War, moreover, was supported so passionately by both sides, including (despite the New York City Draft Riot) Irish-Americans, that one might well question the idea that many Americans, North or South, subscribed to Wells's view about feeding their children (or themselves) to the dogs of war, or that an antiwar song like "Johnny, I Hardly Knew Ye"—unless it were being sung by millions—would need rewriting to shore up morale.

Wells is not alone in his interpretation. But one's skepticism only grows when one discovers that the defiantly pacifist stanza that impresses so many with its seeming historical authority, was created, not by the anonymous Irish "folk" of centuries past, but by California playwright Les Pine, to indict Washington's involvement, not in the Civil War but in the Cold War—and perhaps specifically the Korean War, which began in June, 1950.[10] In the early fifties, New York stage actress and recording artist Martha Schlamme incorporated Pine's work into her performances of "Johnny, I Hardly Knew Ye," notably in a recording for the People's Music "Hootenanny" label (H. 107) in 1952. She performed it again in 1954 on the more widely distributed LP *Folksongs of Many Lands* (Vanguard 7012) as her representative Irish selection. More recently still, British singers, under the spell of a longed-for authenticity, have altered Pine's words to give them an even more "authentic" flavor:

> They're rolling out the guns again
> To go to war in France and Spain
> They never shall have our sons again…[11]

All twentieth-century texts of "Johnny, I Hardly Knew Ye" derive either directly or at one or two removes from that published in 1887 and 1888 by ballad editor H. Halliday Sparling, an associate of the English poet William Morris. Sparling is at pains to say that "This favourite old song is here for the first time given complete." Much of what is known—or assumed—about the song's history comes from this note of Sparling's, expanded in the second edition (1888) from the mere two sentences that appeared in the first the previous year:

> It dates from the beginning of the present century, when Irish regiments were so extensively raised for the East India Service. Because in one late version "Why did you *run* from me and the child" is made "why did you *skedaddle*…" and this word only came into use during the War of Secession, some have imagined this song to be of recent date, and have even attributed it to the Irish-American music-halls! My own memory carries it back to very near the war, when I heard an old fisherman sing it, to whom it was even then old. It was he who told me of its age and meaning, what I have said above, which is corroborated by the reference to Ceylon. It is hard to believe seriously

that any one can read this wonderful piece of grotesquerie, with its mingling of pathos and ribald mockery so closely allied to the spirit that produced "*The Night before Larry was Stretched*" and be unable to see either its value or its genuineness![12]

This is all rather more interesting than informative. Sparling assures us that the old fisherman had told him not many years after the Civil War that he'd known the song for a long time. But Sparling (1860–1924), still in his twenties when he recalled the event, could hardly have been more than ten or twelve years old when the two conversed. And though the singer might well have explained that "Sulloon" was Ceylon, his claim to a child, perhaps simply conjecture or hearsay, that the song was "old" is of no evidentiary value; the same is true of Sparling's assertion that versions containing the humorous word *skedaddle* (which the *Oxford English Dictionary* cannot trace any earlier than 1861) are necessarily "late" and thus artistically and historically misleading.

Sparling's judgment is faulty on another count as well: an apparent reference to Ceylon does not show that the song was created early in the British occupation of that island, now the nation of Sri Lanka. English troops landed in Ceylon in 1795, during the so-called War of the First Coalition, in order to seize French-controlled Dutch settlements.

Native insurgencies against the British occurred in 1803, 1815, and 1817–18. These incidents might argue for a date long before the American Civil War, but the otherwise unidentifiable "Sulloon" may be in the song as no more than a colorful and convenient rhyme. Sparling's footnote suggests that even in 1887 its interpretation as "Ceylon" was not transparent; a previous anthologist, Williams, had simply inserted a question mark after the word. But unlike more dramatic episodes like the Opium Wars (1839–42, 1856–60), the Crimean War (1853–1856), and the Sepoy Rebellion (1857), colonial war in Ceylon was not the kind of struggle likely to inspire the pacifist muse. The British took control of the coastal Dutch forts at a cost of about twenty men killed and wounded, and there were few years between 1796 and 1818 when even a thousand troops were on the island. Army deaths on Ceylon from all causes in the war years 1803, 1815, and 1817–18 totaled

657; as was usual in pre-twentieth century warfare, more soldiers died from disease than from enemy action.

Simply for the sake of perspective: the 657 British deaths from all causes in warfare on Ceylon, during the four calendar years when fighting occurred, were considerably fewer than the 790 Union army deaths in one day of battle at Seven Pines, Virginia, in 1862.[13]

The dramatic and misbegotten charge of the Light Brigade at Balaklava in 1854, resulted in at least one music-hall song ("Cardigan the Fearless") and a famous poem by Tennyson, the Poet Laureate; but the obscure, sporadic, ambush-style warfare in Ceylon seems to have generated no popular or traditional songs, and would seem especially unlikely to have resulted in so apparently bitter an indictment as "Johnny, I Hardly Knew Ye." Certainly there is nothing in any text of the song to link it to any English war in Ceylon or anywhere else.

Sparling unfortunately says nothing about the tune to which he heard the song sung, but because his text is central to later tradition, the words are given here in full:

JOHNNY, I HARDLY KNEW YE
While going the road to sweet Athy,
  Hurroo ! hurroo !
While going the road to sweet Athy,
  Hurroo ! hurroo !
While going the road to sweet Athy,
A stick in my hand and a drop in my eye,
A doleful damsel I heard cry :—
" Och, Johnny, I hardly knew you."
With drums and guns and guns and drums,
  The enemy nearly slew ye,
  My darling dear, you look so queer,
Och, Johnny, I hardly knew ye !

" Where are your eyes that looked so mild ?
  Hurroo ! hurroo !
Where are your eyes that looked so mild ?
  Hurroo ! hurroo !

Where are your eyes that looked so mild,
When my poor heart you first beguiled ?
Why did you run from me and the child ?
       Och, Johnny, I hardly knew ye !"
With drums, etc.

" Where are the legs with which you run ?
       Hurroo ! hurroo !
Where are the legs with which you run ?
       Hurroo ! hurroo !
Where are the legs with which you run,
When you first went to carry a gun ?—
Indeed your dancing days are done !
       Och, Johnny, I hardly knew ye !"
With your drums, etc, [sic]

" It grieved my heart to see you sail,
       Hurroo ! hurroo!
It grieved my heart to see you sail,
       Hurroo ! hurroo !
It grieved my heart to see you sail,
Though from my heart you took leg bail,   ran away *slang*
Like a cod you're doubled up head and tail.
       Och, Johnny, I hardly knew ye !"
With drums, etc.

" You haven't an arm and you haven't a leg,
       Hurroo ! hurroo !
"You haven't an arm and you haven't a leg,
       Hurroo ! hurroo !
You haven't an arm and you haven't a leg,
You're an eyeless, noseless, chickenless egg ;
You'll have to be put in a bowl to beg :
       Och, Johnny, I hardly knew ye !"
With drums, etc.

"I'm happy for to see you home,
        Hurroo ! hurroo !
I'm happy for to see you home,
        Hurroo ! huroo !
I'm happy for to see you home,
All from the island of Sulloon,   Ceylon [Sparling's note][14]
So low in flesh, so high in bone,
        Och, Johnny, I hardly knew ye !
With drums, etc.

" But sad as it is to see you so,
        Hurroo ! hurroo !
But sad as it is to see you so,
        Hurroo ! hurroo !
But sad as it is to see you so,
And to think of you now as an object of woe,
Your Peggy'll still keep ye on as her beau ;
        Och, Johnny, I hardly knew ye ! "

With drums and guns and guns and drums,
        The enemy nearly slew ye,
        My darling dear, you look so queer,
Och, Johnny, I hardly knew ye ! "

(The site of this monologue within a monologue, the market town of Athy, is mentioned early in Joyce's *Portrait of the Artist*: "Why," asks a character, "is the county of Kildare like the leg of a fellow's breeches?" Stephen Dedalus gives up. "Because there's a thigh in it. That's an old riddle."[15])

Thanks to Sparling's interest, the song's literary value, if rarely specified, has often been recognized; its "meaning" and "genuineness," however, are something else. Words almost identical to Sparling's, also without a tune, had appeared in 1881 in Alfred M. Williams's *Poets and Poetry of Ireland*, but Williams's lyrics lack the memorable stanza about the "chickenless egg." Williams was quite as certain as Sparling of the song's age, but his opinion of it differed considerably, and it seems to have been in response to it that Sparling elaborated his own brief note of 1887. According to Williams,

The following is a modern street ballad, as will be seen from the use of the word 'skedaddle,' which was one of the inventions of the American war, and has a strong and graphic humor in spite, or perhaps for the reason, of its uncouth rudeness.[16]

"Humor" is a quality that few singers today claim to detect in the song.

Though the words of "Johnny, I Hardly Knew Ye" were anthologized more than once during the 1890s and after, the song's connection to Gilmore's tune, "When Johnny Comes Marching Home," was not made explicit until 1903, when the Irish-American tune collector Francis O'Neill printed the familiar melody as both "Johnny, Fill Up the Bowl" and "Johnny, I Hardly Knew You" (sic), which is indexed as an alternative title. O'Neill's melody, however, comprises only sixteen bars, with no room for the four-line chorus included by both Sparling and Williams; this O'Neill rectified with the addition of eight more bars in 1922, when he also accepted "Johnny, I Hardly Knew You" as the tune's primary title.[17]

In 1915, during the First World War, Charlotte Milligan Fox, the prime mover of the Irish Folk Song Society, arranged a version of Sparling's text, set to Gilmore's tune of "When Johnny Comes Marching Home." Fox's publication also contained the Irish street ballad of "Mistress Magrath"[sic], described rather oddly as a "recruiting song," though it too focuses on the homecoming of a legless soldier, which it treats with a combination of dismay and broad humor ("Or was it walking in the sea/ Wore your two fine legs from the knees away?")[18] The next publication of both words and music, in Irish composer Herbert Hughes's *Irish Country Songs* III (1934), was accompanied by the editor's peculiar, but nonetheless informative, discussion. Hughes, born in Belfast in 1882, was more than twenty years Sparling's junior and thus even farther removed from the debated period of the song's origin. His version of the text consists of Sparling's stanzas 1, 2, 3, and 6, with the chorus expanded into stanza length as in the Clancy-Makem version. To Sparling's note Hughes adds his own recollections:

It is a song that I have remembered since I was a child sung in Ireland to the tune of 'Johnny comes marching home,' which tune has appeared in popular collections as 'old English.' When I first thought of putting it in this volume, I discussed the song with my father, who is in his eighty-second year, with Mr. Henry W. Nevinson, Dr. John S. Crone, and others whose memories went back to the American Civil War, or a little after. Without being dogmatic, they agreed that it belonged to that period and came from the States, Sir Richard Terry remarking that it was probably in the repertory of the Christy Minstrels.

Despite this attribution of the song by several observers to a time no earlier than the 1860s, with a suggestion, perhaps, of an American origin, Hughes remains emotionally committed to Sparling's attribution of the song to a much earlier period. Though his tone suggests some significant recent discovery, he adds nothing new as he confidently endorses Sparling's opinion of its origin:

> [F]urther research dated it back, conjecturally, to the peri-od immediately succeeding the Treaty of Amiens in 1802, when, as H. H. Sparling pointed out, Irish regiments were extensively recruited for the East India service.[19]

No evidence seems to exist that recruiting for "Irish regiments," such as the 18th (The Royal Irish) Regiment of Foot, was especially vigorous after 1802, or that more Irishmen served in Ceylon than anywhere else. (By 1840, Irishmen made up more than 40 percent of the entire British army, though the proportion had dropped to 28 percent in 1870.[20] In any event, Hughes' reasoning is no sounder than Sparling's: knowing no better, one might equally say that "research" has dated the popular song "Deep in the Heart of Texas" (John Swander and June Hershey, 1942) "back, conjecturally," to the 1830s or '40s, because Texas was then much in the news—more in the U.S. than Ceylon had been in Britain.

Thus for Sparling and Hughes (if not for Williams), "Johnny, I Hardly Knew Ye" was a curious antique, a survival of some early Ceylonese military campaign; yet, if that were the case, how explain its sudden popularity in Ireland in the 1860s, even if it had presumably been brought back from America, where it must have survived quite invisibly until it was discovered and rewritten by Patrick Gilmore? Hughes's faith in this improbable story is especially remarkable, for to him goes the credit for finding the most significant piece of the puzzle, though he is stubbornly resolved not to see its significance. In light of the frequent assertion that the song originated as a cry of antiwar anguish in Ireland around 1800, it should be emphasized that every singer or scholar who has consulted Hughes's essay has had this passage before his or her eyes; but all those who subsequently have written about the song have chosen simply to ignore it. Hughes writes:

> ...I discovered that a song with the same title, with "words and music by J. B. Geoghegan," had been published in London about 1867, and "sung with tremendous applause by Harry Liston, the star comic." The words of Mr. Geoghegan's song were substantially the same as those recorded by Mrs. Fox, but the tune, while recalling that of "Johnny comes marching home," was definitely an inferior one.

Hughes then reprints Geoghegan's mixolydian melody, which bears some resemblance to Gilmore's in both contour and feeling. But Hughes goes on to exercise his ingenuity to show that the *song itself* must be older than "about 1867," which is near indeed to "the American Civil War or a little after," precisely the period to which both Sparling's memory and Hughes's father and friends assigned it:

> The resemblance between the tune printed above and "Johnny comes marching home" is such that one is tempted to assume that Geoghegan's memory was at fault. The practice of setting music-hall doggerel to traditional tunes without acknowledgment is not, of course, uncommon, and has been profitably developed by more than one famous comedian of our own day.... Is it too much to suppose that the late Mr. Geoghegan, with the music-hall mind of his epoch, considered that a good old ballad was anybody's property? The sentiment created on both sides of the Atlantic by the War of Secession was certainly worth exploiting. Thus far, then, my friends had good excuse for associating the song with that epoch.

But "thus far" is as far as it goes. There is no doubt whatever that Gilmore's own song and its stirring melody gained immense popularity in America during the Civil War and was soon printed on broadsides in England, where it became a hit as well. That a music-hall composer like Geoghegan could have so unreliable a memory for tunes that he would imperfectly recollect the new and popular "When Johnny Comes Marching Home" is impossible to credit. Hughes's argument appears to be that Geoghegan "must have" set new "music-hall doggerel" to an old tune, to exploit the recent American Civil War: yet he also seems to say that the words themselves go back "conjecturally" to around 1803. This seems very much like nonsense

Hughes's description of the original sheet music is also telling:

> The cover-design of this publication of the sixties was in colour, pretty in its conventional way, showing the dolorous damsel with her hair nicely parted in the middle, complete with shawl, pinafore, and a pair of elegant shoes on incredibly small feet. She is making a gesture of surprise before a heavily mustachioed soldier who is clad in red tunic and dark trousers, and wearing the high infantry cap of the time, with an eye-guard over one eye, an arm in a sling, and one leg doubled up on a short crutch.[21]

The British Library holds what appears to be the unique repository copy of Geoghegan's sheet music, deposited in February, 1867. Johnny's red coat is enough to show that the song has no connection to the Civil War concluded nearly two years earlier in America, a war between the blue and the gray in which no British troops were involved.

Joseph Bryan Geoghegan, the credited lyricist and composer of "Johnny, I Hardly Knew Ye," was a successful English music-hall songwriter and theater manager, born on Oldfield Road, Salford, Manchester, on April 13, 1815. From 1864 to his death on January 21, 1889, he was manager of the Victoria Music Hall in Bolton, and was for a time proprietor of the Star Theatre in Hanley. He is said to have written or composed some two hundred songs during his career. One whose popularity may have exceeded that of "Johnny, I Hardly Knew Ye" (or "Know Ye" as the cover of the 1867 sheet music inconsistently has it) is the burlesque sea song "Ten Thousand Miles

Away" (1870) with its jocular line, "I'm off to my love with a boxing glove." The third of Geoghegan's greatest hits was "Down in a Coal Mine" (1872).[22] All in all, about forty songs with words or music credited to Geoghegan can be identified in period songsters and the sheet music collection of the British Library.

There will be more to say about lyrics later, but we should turn for a moment to the melody of "When Johnny Comes Marching Home" and Patrick S. Gilmore's connection to it. Isn't it true that Patrick Sarsfield Gilmore (1829–1892) was born on Christmas Day near Dublin and raised in Ballygar, Co. Galway? And, as has so often been said, didn't he merely exploit a traditional Irish tune (with a structure identical to that of "Johnny, I Hardly Knew Ye"), and fit it out for what Wells calls "propaganda" with new, "pro-war" words (as Doniger would have it)?

The indisputably Irish Gilmore settled permanently in Boston as a young man in 1849, where he successively became the leader of several popular brass bands. A proficient composer and cornetist, he was hired by P. T. Barnum in 1851 for the promotional tour of Jenny Lind, the soprano, acclaimed as the "Swedish Nightingale." So successful did Gilmore's Salem Band become that they were invited to play at the inauguration of President James Buchanan in Washington, D.C., in March, 1857. Shortly after the outbreak of civil war in April, 1861, the thirty-one-year old Gilmore enrolled with his entire Grand Boston Band in the 24th Massachusetts Volunteer Infantry, and he was eventually made bandmaster of all Massachusetts volunteer regiments by Governor John Andrew. In 1864 Union General Nathaniel Banks appointed Gilmore bandmaster of the Department of the Gulf, headquartered in New Orleans. Gilmore became prominent during and after the war as the organizer of amazing outdoor concerts utilizing tens of thousands of instrumentalists and singers, one of which was the International Peace Jubilee in Boston in 1872; his obituary in at least one Irish-American newspaper took up a full seven columns.[23]

The first sheet-music publication of "When Johnny Comes Marching Home" was deposited for copyright in the Library of Congress on September 26, 1863, with words and music credited to "Louis Lambert." Why Gilmore chose to publish under a pseudonym is not clear, but popular composers of the period often employed *noms de plume*, or simply their initials, to add a touch of romantic "mystery" to their product. Copyright on the song was retained by the publishers, Henry Tolman & Co., of Boston.

In an 1883 article in the *Musical Herald*, Gilmoreforthrightly declined to take credit for composing the famous melody to "When Johnny Comes Marching Home":

> [The tune] was a musical waif which I happened to hear somebody humming in the early days of the rebellion, and taking a fancy to it, wrote it down, dressed it up, gave it a name, and rhymed it into usefulness for a special purpose suited to the times.[24]

Gilmore gives no indication that the presumably anonymous tune had any words attached to it or, if it had, that he'd taken any interest in them. It is usually assumed that the tune Gilmore heard was Irish. Many years after the Civil War, for example, the Hon. John C. Linehan, a locally prominent, Irish-born former officer of the 17th New Hampshire Volunteers, casually described Gilmore's tune as "a rollicking old Irish air."[25] The 1903 printing of the tune by Francis O'Neill has already been mentioned: O'Neill believed the air to be Irish, but he gave no evidence for why he thought so.

Had Gilmore never admitted to borrowing the tune, the claim that "Johnny, I Hardly Knew Ye" was some kind of suppressed original might never have been made. Music historian James R. Fuld sought diligently but inconclusively for antecedents of Gilmore's hexatonic melody, but it seems to bear, after all, no objectively "Irish" features. Any alleged "Irishness" seems to result mainly from five associations:

1. Gilmore himself was an Irishman; he wrote frankly that his famous tune was not entirely original with him, so perhaps it was Irish.

2. The sprightliness of Gilmore's 6/8 march is expressed somewhat paradoxically in the "dark" or "sad" dorian mode, a combination not uncommon in Irish dance music.

3. The 1863 sheet music of "When Johnny Comes Marching Home" includes introductory measures which are nearly identical to the second part of the eighteenth-century Scots-Irish jig, "Bung Your Eye," whose melody

is much like that of the Irish-American "Lanigan's Ball," which was widely played by Civil War musicians.

4. Many texts of the Irish song, "Shule Agrah," have the refrain, "Johnny has gone for a soldier." So presumably his homecoming song must be Irish too.

5. Alan Lomax, in *Folk Songs of North America* (1960), notes that his colleague, Seamus Ennis, points the tune's similarity to the Irish *Pretty Girl Milking a Cow.*[26]

Of these observations, only the first, second, and fifth have any logical bearing on the tune's provenance, but even all together they afford thin evidence indeed. First, Gilmore heard the original melody hummed in America, not in Ireland, and gives no indication that he suspected that it had an Irish origin.

Second, the Belfast-born Herbert Hughes seems to have been content with the suggestion that the tune was really "old English." Third, no reported traditional melody to the well-known Irish sentimental song named by Ennis ("The Pretty Girl Milking Her Cow") seems to bear any resemblance to Gilmore's, whose mode and stanzaic form differ from it completely. And finally, Fuld cites the opinion of the Irish musicologist Donal O'Sullivan that he "does not consider the melody of 'When Johnny Comes Marching Home' as Irish in origin."[27] Thus the claim for the clear "Irishness" of Gilmore's tune and Geoghegan's seems to lack any historical basis, and its general acceptance as fact has benefited greatly through repetition. There is simply no way of telling where the tune originated. And, even if it could be determined, is the country of the melody's origin of any significance except to people of a very romantic turn of mind? One feels that the answer is no.

Fuld's research, however, takes us one step farther back than Gilmore. Fuld discovered that the famous melody had been published under the title "Johnny Fill Up the Bowl," by John J. Daly, 419 Grand St., New York City, "about July, 1863," two or three months before the publication of "When Johnny Comes Marching Home." Fuld goes on to say,

> ...[t]he sheet music has an 1863 copyright claim, but, strangely, there is no entry of an 1863 copyright deposit in the copyright records at [the Library of Congress]. The

plate number 167 indicates publication about July 1, 1863 [number 166 having appeared at the end of June and 176 early in August].[28]

"Johnny, Fill Up the Bowl," of course, is how O'Neill titled the melody in 1903. Consistent with Fuld's calculation of a printed appearance in mid-1863 is that the partly topical stanzas of "Johnny Fill Up the Bowl" take current events no further than the loss of the ironclad USS *Monitor* off Cape Hatteras on December 31, 1862; there is no mention, for example, of the Union defeat at Chancellorsville in May, 1863, or the dramatic Union victories at Gettysburg and Vicksburg early in July. The copy of the original sheet music at the Library of Congress shows that, but for accidentals, the printed melody, "arranged," not composed, "by J. Durnal," is unmistakably that of "When Johnny Comes Marching Home."

Because of the historical significance of "Johnny Fill Up the Bowl," which was frequently refitted with new words by soldiers and other publishers, on both sides of the Mason-Dixon line, the original , less-than-inspired lyrics are given below:

> A Soldier I'm just from the war
> Foot balls, Foot balls
> A Soldier I'm just from the war
> Foot balls, says I
> A Soldier I'm just from the war
> Where thundering guns and cannons roar
> And we'll all drink stone blind
> Johnny fill up the bowl
>
> CHORUS
> And we'll all drink stone blind
> Johnny fill up the bowl
>
> I've been in many a bully fight...
> And I'll tell you about a few tonight...
> And we'll all &c.

At first they led us to Bull Run,...
But "changed our base" for Washington...

The rebels came to Maryland,...
A ragged, rough and hungry band...

They didn't have much time to stay,...
For we fought them night and day;...

Old Stonewall Jackson and his crew,...
We made "Nip up de do den do!"...

For bravely did our little Mac,...
Make them take the backward track;...

There was a man went to the war,...
The greatest fool you ever saw;...

He had a hat but ne'er a coat,...
So he buttoned his pantaloons up to his throat!...

The ladies fell in love with him,...
His maiden name I think was Jim;...

To the camp meeting we did go,...
And floured the niggers white as snow;...

You ought to see them sing and jump,...
And chase the Old Boy round a stump;...

The woods with shout and chorus rang,...
And this was one of the songs they sang,...

The Merrimac was all the talk,...
But the little Monitor made her walk!...

And though the Monitor's days are o'er,…
Where she came from there's plenty more!…

John Bull don't like our Iron-clads,…
Nor Frenchy our Columbiads!…

They make them feel so very queer,…
I hardly think they'll interfere;…[29]

The date established by Fuld for this piece makes it probable that Gilmore borrowed the tune of "When Johnny Comes Marching Home" from someone who was humming the *tune* Daly and Durnal called "Johnny, Fill Up the Bowl"—regardless of any song text that it may have carried. Indeed, a color-illustrated, undated slip of Gilmore's lyrics, printed by his own Boston publisher, actually states that "When Johnny Comes Marching Home" should be sung to the air of "Johnny Fill Up the Bowl." But, as we will see, the tune was very unlikely to have originated on Grand Street in New York.

As others have noted, there is also a marked melodic resemblance between the Durnal-Gilmore "Johnny" tune and that of Burns's song "John Anderson, My Jo," which was very familiar to parlor musicians of the nineteenth century. The tunes may fairly be described as first cousins. Though the Scottish tune, which first appears in the Skene Ms. of *ca* 1630, and so is essentially contemporary with that of "The Three Ravens," may have directly inspired "Johnny, Fill Up the Bowl," I believe that the Irish musicologist Donal O'Sullivan identified the earliest source many years ago.[30]

Fuld cites O'Sullivan as positing the seventeenth-century ballad of the "Three Ravens" (Child 26) in Ravenscroft's *Melismata* (1611) as the earliest ancestor of the "Johnny" tune; Fuld, however, saw "no substantial resemblance."[31] But his feeling for "substantial resemblance" between melodies likely to have been learned and relearned by ear over many generations may have been insensitive in this case. "The Three Ravens" may or may not have been strictly traditional—as Bronson suggests, Ravenscroft may have modernized an earlier "pure Dorian" melody—but the stanzaic form is unquestionably that of the "Johnny" songs, as well as of the ribald "Hinky-Dinky Parlez-Vous" of the First World War and its entirely bawdy progenitor, "The German Officers Crossed the Rhine."

More than the stanzaic form, however, indicates a kinship between the rowdy "Johnny Fill Up the Bowl" of the nineteenth century and the dirge-like, oddly mystical "Three Ravens" of the seventeenth. Leisy (195) makes O'Sullivan's suggested line of descent tangible simply by observing the near identity between the three opening measures of "When Johnny"/ "Fill Up the Bowl" and Frank Kidson's traditional version of the "Ravens." Kidson (17) (not, as Leisy says, "Chappell") relates that his informant, "Mr. John Holmes of Roundhay," learned "The Three Ravens" "about 1825 from his mother's singing… in a remote village among the Derbyshire hills, most aptly named Stony Middleton."

Holmes thus learned a tune clearly related to that of "Johnny" in England more than three decades before the American Civil War. Indeed, much of Holmes's pentatonic melody, if put into 6/8 time and given an additional tone, would strikingly resemble that of "Johnny Fill Up the Bowl."

These plausible tune relationships also suggest an explanation for the curious but widespread refrain of *footballs, for balls*, and the like, in texts of "Johnny, Fill Up the Bowl." In 1901, Elizabeth Duane Gillespie recalled a song she'd heard from a young man near Pensacola, Florida, in 1853. All she could say about the tune, however, was that it was "queer" and must have carried "at least twenty verses." What makes Gillespie's song relevant, besides its early date and familiar stanzaic form, is its combination of nonsense refrains that might have evolved into something like "Foot balls, foot balls"; there is also the striking coincidence of both "John" and "all drink stone blind" in the last line of the chorus. There are plenty of "Johns" in folksong, but this is the only known occurrence of "all drink stone blind" outside of "Johnny Fill Up the Bowl" that I'm aware of:

'I saw a flea hew a tree, boo, boo,
I saw a flea hew a tree, boo for John,
I saw a flea hew a tree ten miles in the sea,
Let us all drink stone blind, boo for John.

'I saw a pig run a mile, boo, boo,
I saw a pig run a mile, boo for John,
I saw a pig run a mile with a little fat hen [sic
Let us all, etc.

'I saw a hen bil' a pen, boo, boo,   [sic

I saw a hen bil' a pen, boo for John,

I saw a hen bil' a pen with a hatchet in her hand,

Let us all, etc. [34]

With a less bibulous refrain, this song has become "Fooba Wooba John," popularized by Burl Ives in the late 1940s. And of course, too, it is an American reflex of the Scots drinking song "Wha's Fu'? Wha's Fu'?" One conjectures that "Boo, boo!" "Fooba Wooba!" and "Foot balls! Foot balls!" have all descended from a Scots refrain like "Fu' bowl! Fu' bowl!" (The meaningless "Boo for John" might then have been "A bowl for John," hence "Johnny Fill Up the Bowl.") The suggestion is made a little more likely by Geordie MacIntyre's discovery in Scotland in the early 1960s of a version of "Wha's Fu'?" sung to a tune that seems to partake of both "When Johnny" and "John Anderson." The singer, Arthur Lochhead of Paisley (1892–1975), seems to have learned it in the early part of the twentieth century.[35]

The following tunes have been transposed to end on A. Stuart's "John Anderson" is for the flute, and the notation of Gilmore's melody includes the often omitted introductory passage based on the jig "Bung Your Eye":

1611
The Three Ravens (Ravenscroft)

ca 1630
John Anderson my Jo (Skene Ms.)

ca 1726
John Anderson, My Jo (Stuart)

1782
John Anderson My Jo (Aird)

ca 1825
The Three Ravens (Holmes/Kidson)

1863
Johnny, Fill Up the Bowl

When Johnny Comes Marching Home (Gilmore)

Johnny, I Hardly Knew Ye (Geoghegan)

Wha's Fu'? (Lochhead)

That the "Ravens" tune of 1611 was the single direct ancestor of those that followed is unlikely, but Holmes's melody does appear to show similarities to what came before as well as what came after. Unlike "Johnny, Fill Up the Bowl," there is certainly nothing humorous in Holmes's "Ravens," the text of which belongs to the ballad's tragical stage, and Holmes's mother in Derbyshire may have been one of the last singers within that mostly un-written tradition. As ballad scholars are aware, however, comically ghoulish versions of the "Ravens," transformed into "Three Crows" and sometimes featuring a raucous refrain of "Billy Magee Magaw," have been collected many times in the United States. Such versions are usually sung to tunes essentially the same as that of "Johnny Fill Up the Bowl" in Durnal's or Gilmore's interpretations. Proof that that same tune, or something a bit closer to it than Holmes's, actually carried "Three Crows" in America during the Civil War remains elusive, but there is evidence to suggest that it did. Linehan, for example, the Union officer who thought Gilmore's was a "rollicking old Irish air," goes on to write that,

> the boys… added several verses, a little "off color" from
> a prohibition standpoint, and used to sing them with a
> vigor that would please the author of the original:

> For we'll all drink stone blind
> When Johnnie comes marching home.

….It was a very dull crowd around campfire or at mess that [sic] the old songs of home were not heard, "Saw my leg off short,"adapted to the well known air of "Greeneville;" "Old Grimes is dead, that good old man," "There were three crows sat on a tree," etc.[36]

The ghoulish incarnation of "The Three Crows," with its dead horse on the plain was so familiar at Yale during the period that W.A. Linn, '68, was prompted to contribute a burlesque exegesis of it to the *Yale Literary Magazine* (Sample: "Surely no one will lisp aught against this noble trio").[37] Moreover, an 1886 song collection designed to wake the nostalgia of Minnesota veterans prints, along with "Dixie's Land," "Tramp, Tramp, Tramp," and other Civil War favorites, "Crow Song" with "Billy Magee, Magaw!" choruses.[38] Kittredge cites printings in 1863 and '64 without providing the texts.[39] Bates, Parker, and Chapman (1875) print a collegiate parody of the "Crow Song" ("There were three Sophs sat on a fence,/ Billy Mc Gee Mc Gaw") with directions that it be sung to "When Johnny Comes Marching Home."[40]

It is impossible to know just when or where "Three Ravens" tunes—like that sung in Derbyshire in the 1820s—became virtually indistinguishable from that of "Johnny Fill Up the Bowl"/"When Johnny Comes Marching Home." But Linehan's recollection that both "Johnny" and the "Crows" were sung around the same Civil War campfires, and the appearance of the "Crow Song" in the Minnesota veterans' song book strongly indicates that the melodic identity of "Johnny" and "The Three Crows" was complete for many singers by the end of he Civil War, in the spring of 1865.[41]

We should now turn to the lyrics and reception of "Johnny, I Hardly Knew Ye." We should also recapitulate the associated legend that "Johnny, I Hardly Knew Ye" arose as an anonymous song in Ireland in the late eighteenth or early nineteenth century, as a powerful "folk protest" against English rule and the ruthless conscription of the Irish poor to fight in brutal, colonial wars, as in Ceylon. (The earliest attributed and unsupported date I have seen is "the 1760s"; Linebaugh connects it to some unnamed "battle" of the mid-eighteenth century.[42]) Yet it should now be evident that every premise of that folksong legend is false. The words of "Johnny, I Hardly Knew Ye," along with an original melody that has fallen from use, were written not in Ireland but in England, not long before February, 1867, by Joseph B. Geoghegan, a prolific English songwriter and successful music-hall figure. It remains now to examine the song's lyrical variations and their changing interpretations.

The appearance of Geoghegan's song in Alfred Perceval Graves's 1884 anthology, *Songs of Irish Wit and Humour* should be enough to warn us that the typical nineteenth-century music-hall audience may have felt differently about the song than audiences today, particularly when they saw it performed on stage by Harry Liston, "the star English comic."[43] When Alfred Williams praised the song in 1881, it was not for its sentiments but for its "strong and graphic humour in spite, or perhaps for the reason, of its rude uncouthness." Williams' text is much like Sparling's, but it lacks two stanzas that Williams may have suppressed for reasons of taste: the allusion to the "chickenless egg" and the finale in which a suddenly contrite Peggy promises to keep Johnny "on as her beau," a "happy" ending, to be sure— but with the unmistakable innuendo (highly objectionable to middle-class sensibilities) that their child is illegitimate.[44]

Here, reprinted for the first time, is Geoghegan's 1867 text from the British Library. (My sincere thanks go to Steve Roud for supplying a scan of the words.) The first stanza was printed in full under the music, but to save space it is then repeated, as below, in condensed form with the succeeding stanzas; the bracketed words below show it in full. Note the stage-Irish spelling of *wid* for "with" and the use of *ye*'s as a typically "illiterate" Irish singular pronoun. Another clear music-hall trait is the return of the narrator's voice in the final stanza, an indication that the song was written to accompany some sort of skit:

JOHNNY, I HARDLY KNEW YE

I.
When on the road to old Athy, ahoo! [ahoo!
When on the road to old Athy, ahoo! ahoo!
When on the road to old Athy,
The harvest moon was in the sky;
I heard a dolorous damsel cry—
Och ! Johnny, I hardly knew ye!

Chorus.
Wid drums and guns, and guns and drums,
The enemy fairly slew ye;
My darling dear, ye look so queer—
Och ! Johnny, I hardly knew ye.

II.
Where is your nose, ye pitiful crow, ahoo!
Ye had it when ye went to scatter the foe,
The loss of it has disfigured ye so—
Och ! Johnny, I hardly knew ye.

III.
Where is your eye that looked so wild, ahoo!
When my poor heart ye first beguiled;
Why did you skedaddle from me and the child—
Och! Johnny I hardly knew ye.

Wid drums and guns, &c.

IV.
It broke my heart to see ye sail, [sic]
And seeing ye here would raise a wail—
The cut of your head would embellish a tale—[sic]
Och ! Johnny, I hardly knew ye.

Wid drums and guns, &c.

V.
Where are the legs wid which ye run, ahoo!
When first ye went to shoulder a gun;
I fear your dancing days are done—
Och! Johnny, I hardly knew ye.

Wid drums and guns, &c.

VI.

Ye haven't an arm, Ye haven't a leg, ahoo
You're a noseless, eyeless, chickenless egg
Ye'll have to be put in a bowl to beg
Och! Johnny I hardly knew ye.

Wid drums & guns, &c.

VII

But sad as it is to see you so, ahoo!
And to think of you now as an object of woe,
Your Peggy will still keep ye on as her beau,
Though, Johnny, she hardly knew ye.

Wid drums & guns, &c.[45]

In Ireland, ballad-slips printed by P. Brereton of Dublin in the late 1860s must have furthered the song's popularity. (The Bodleian Library dates them to "ca 1867.") The slips indicate no tune, and Brereton's version is even more self-consciously grotesque than Geoghegan's. The printing is especially poor, so I have silently corrected the many missing and inverted letters: otherwise the text is *ad litteram*. Even if it could be shown—as it cannot—that Brereton's Dublin text actually predates Geoghegan's, and, as a putatively anonymous song, represents more truly the "voice of the folk," that voice, in this case, does not protest war: instead it revels in a mad compound of humor—whimsical, sardonic, mildly erotic, sadistic, and finally, perhaps, tender:

JOHNEY [sic] I HARDLY KNEW YE

While going the road to sweet Athy Hurroo! Hurroo!
While going the road to sweet Athy Hurroo!
While going the road to sweet Athy with a stick
…in my hand and a drop in my eye,
A doleful damsel I heard cry
Jonney I hardly knew ye!

CHORUS
With your drums & guns & guns & drums
The enemy nearly slew ye
O darling dear you look so queer
Faith Jonny I hardly knew ye.

Where are your eyes that looked so mild hurroo!
Where are your eyes that looked so mild hurroo!
Where are your eyes that looked so mild
...when my heart you did begile,
Why did you skedaddle from me and the child why
...Johney I hardly knew ye

O where's your arms too alack huroo
O where's your arms too alack huroo
O where's your arms too alack I often
...felt them on my back
From pain I roar'd at every crack
...O Jonney it's then I knew ye

Where are the legs with which you run hurroo!
Where are the legs with which you run hurroo!
Where are the legs with which you run
...when you went to carry a gun,
Indeed your dancing days are done faith
...Johney I hardly knew ye

It grieved my heart to see you sail hurroo!
It grieved my heart to see you sail hurroo!
It grieved my heart to see you sail
...if my heart you felt you would bewail,
I shook my head like the tail of a whale
...Jonny I hardly knew ye,

I'll tell you the truth without controul huroo!
I'll tell you the truth without controul
I'll tell you the truth without coutroul
…your atitude looks very droll,
Young as long & as thin as a tellagraph pole
…O Jonney I hardly knew you,

O where's the whiskdr[sic] you aught to have there hurroo
O where's the whisker you aught to have there hurroo
O where's the whisker you aught to have there
…I'm sure your jaws looks very bare,
You only were fit to throw in the rere [sic]
…O Jonny I hardly knew you,

But still I'm glad to see you home hurroo,
But still I'm glad to see you home hurroo,
But still I'm glad to see you home from the Iland of saloam
Your so low in flesh & high in bone
… faith Jonney I hardly knew you.[46]

Quite in fitting with the anarchic tone, Geoghegan's harvest moon in the sky is replaced with "a drop in my eye," the phrase which supplants it in every later text until recent singers, anticipating the grief to come, began singing "a tear in my eye." But, as the OED makes clear, a "drop in one's eye" refers not to tears of grief but to "signs of having had a glass;" that is, being bleary-eyed from drink. In Brereton's and derived texts, the narrator is as tipsy as any comic stage Irishman. The soldier's sudden absence of "whiskers" seems to imply a castratory wound as well, suggesting that the broadside writer sensed clearly the castration anxiety that may underlie some of the humor even in Geoghegan's lyrics; "fit" only to be thrown "in the rear" of the army implies being unable to fight, perhaps even from the start. With its eavesdropping narrator, distracted young woman, and returned lover, the song's entire situation, moreover, recalls that of the ubiquitous "Dark-Eyed Sailor" (Roud 265), one of the most frequently-encountered English street ballads of the nineteenth-century, which, known as early as 1847, had thus been familiar for many years.[47]

An indication of the influence of Brereton's broadside is that it contains the seed of the now customary reference to the "island of Sulloon," which was absent from Geoghegan's version. Williams (1881), whose source is unknown, was mystified by what he spells as "Sulloon"; Graves (1884) rationalized the word to "Ceylon," and he was followed in this by Sparling (1887) and many more since. Certainly a broadside parodist may have had Ceylon in mind without knowing how to spell it. But whatever the intention, "saloom" on the broadside is at least reminiscent of the Pool of Siloam, near Jerusalem, to which Jesus sends the blind man for healing (John 9:6). The broadside versifier seems thus to have found an unusually suggestive rhyme, which may or may not have anything to do with "Ceylon."

There is one more variant pattern, on sheets printed by Such of London before 1885 and Pearson of Manchester some time before 1900, according to the Bodleian; the two texts are virtually identical and follow Sparling in all but a word or two up to the final stanzas:

JOHNNY, I HARDLY KNEW YE

In my heart you left a wail,
You have scarce a head, what a sorrowful tale,
Oh, Johnny, I hardly knew ye.

I've just gone through a long campaign,
It's true, it's true,
Far better for me had I been slain,
It's true, it's true,
When I enter the town of sweet Athy,
With two wooden stumps, and a patch on my eye,
And worse than all, without telling a lie,
Oh, Molly is going to leave me.

Through the wars and scars, the scars & wars,
I thought she'd never deceive me
By the whiskers I wear, this world is quare,
And Molly is going to leave me.[48]

That the Such/Pearson version adds the pathos of lost love to the original (and is not the original itself) is indicated by its incongruously tacked-on quality, which contrasts with the amusingly tipsy narrator and the punning on *head and tail*.

One of Tolman's Civil War printings of Gilmore's "When Johnny Comes Marching Home" calls it "a song for home, the camp, and the concert room"; the blurb testifies, truly it would seem, to the lively song's tremendous popularity: "It is sung and performed with unbounded success nightly, at the entertainments of all the Minstrel Troupes, Old Folks Troupes, and the Hutchinson Family, Gilmore's Band, etc."[49] By the time when Geoghegan's song was published, in 1867, Gilmore's was a transatlantic hit. This was partly through the success of George W. Moore's blackface Christy's (formerly Pierce's) Minstrels. (It is difficult to determine precisely who was singing what, because several different minstrel troupes were using the name "Christy's Minstrels.") Moore's performance of "When Johnny Comes Marching Home" at the Music Hall in Edinburgh on January 21, 1865, was greeted with "tremendous applause."[50] At Queen's Hall in Liverpool on May 1, Moore delivered the song "with irresistible drollery, and a burlesque duet between himself and Mr. Crocker, in imitation of Scotch bagpipes, convulsed the audience with laughter."[51] The Bodleian alone holds no fewer than twenty-six copies of the song issued by American, Scottish, and English printers.

Geoghegan's creation seems to parody "When Johnny Comes Marching Home" not for any idealistic, antiwar purpose but for the sheer brutal fun of it. There is also the interesting matter of the song's refrain: *ahoo!* in Geoghegan and *hurroo!* almost everywhere else. As an interjection in English, "Ahoo!" is almost unique, but Geoghegan may have gotten it from a blackface song that contains a touch of similarly sadistic humor:

Ahoo! Ahoo!
A PLANTATION DANCE,

Old fat Sam died ob decline,
Ahoo, ahoo, oo, ool
And dey dried him for a 'bacco sign
Ahoo, ahoo, oo, oo![52]

Geoghegan's "Ahoo!" was quickly replaced in Irish broadsheet printings with the more conventional "Hurroo!" which modern singers interpret as an expression of grief or solicitude. All historical evidence, however, shows that interpretation to be in error. The OED, with examples from 1824 and 1891, defines *hurroo* as "A cry expressive of triumph or exultant excitement;" in other words, a Hibernian equivalent of *hurrah!* or *hooray!* entirely consistent with the line, "I'm happy for to see you home," as well as with the repeated *hurrahs!* of "When Johnny Comes Marching Home." Nineteenth-century sources show that it also functioned much as *hey!* or even *hello!* [53]

The earliest datable notice of "Johnny I Hardly Knew Ye" in Ireland seems to be that in *Freeman's Journal and Daily Commercial Advertiser* (Dublin) July 6, 1867;[54] the song appears to have been inserted for comic relief into a production of Goethe's *Faust*. On September 2, 1867, the same paper advertised the appearance of Burton's "Christy's Minstrels" at the Rotundo Rooms on Dublin's Cavendish Row: this appearance confirms the recollection of Hughes's elderly consultants.

On THIS DAY (Monday), 2nd September—
And EVERY EVENING, At Eight o'Clock.
Under the distinguished patronage of
His Excellency the MARQUIS of ABERCORN, K.G., Lord Lieutenant
ENTIER [sic] CHANGE OF PROGRAMME—
Including the following ORIGINAL SONGS,
Music and Words,
To be had at Messrs. Sinclair & Co. Marlborough-street, London:
"I heard a Spirit Sing;" "Mill May"
"Johnny, I Hardly Knew You."

BURTON'S
Great American Troupe of
CHRISTY'S MINSTRELS,
The best concentration of Comedians and Vocalists in the world!!![55]

Of the three titles mentioned, clearly intended to be typical of the troupe's offerings, only "Johnny" is likely to have furnished material for the "best… Comedians… in the world."

Early in September, the song was heard on the streets of Cork and was mentioned derisively:

> "Last week a laughable incident occurred in George's street, Cork. One of those modern minnesingers, whose *chansons de canailles* chanted from halfpenny broadsheets have been making night hideous for some time past in our thoroughfares, while vociferating with more spirit than melody that popular song, 'Johnny, I hardly knew you,' and while dwelling on the most thrilling note of his refrain, startled the knot of admiring listeners who surrounded him by changing from a pathetic *basso-profundo* to an *alto* as wild and piercing as it was unexpected. His repeated shrieks at last died away in a howl of mortal agony, and dropping his ballad he limped along… writhing and jumping like a man possessed." The reason: he had been stung on the lip by a wasp, "thus making a decisive hole in his ballad." It was a "stinging rebuke."[56]

Quoting the *Cork Examiner*, the *Newcastle Courant* ("Ecclesiastical Intelligence), reported that on September 5, the Wesleyan missionary, the Rev. Mr. Campbell, had been ridiculed at an open-air sermon in Ireland "as he was adapting a Wesleyan hymn to the popular strains of 'Pop Goes the Weasel.'" The crowd, "as a counter attraction, struck up, we believe, 'Johnny, I hardly knew you,' a popular ballad of the satirical class."[57]

On August 15, 1868, the Poet's Box, a Glasgow broadside printer, listed the song as one of their "newest."[58] The records show, perhaps predictably, that Harry Liston, the English comedian that Sir Richard Terry still associated many decades later with "Johnny, I Hardly Knew Ye," had both Gilmore's and Geoghegan's compositions in his extensive repertoire: The London sheet-music publication of "When Johnny Comes Marching Home" advertises it as "sung by the Christy Minstrels and by Harry Liston."[59] Liston's alternating performances—possibly in sequence to enhance the incongruity—may have helped to encourage the singing of Geoghegan's words to Gilmore's melody. Liston is described as he performed "Johnny, I Hardly Knew Ye" in Bangor in 1869:

MR. LISTON'S CONCERTS.—The entertainments by Mr Harry Liston on Saturday and Monday evenings drew crowded audiences, the Penrhyn Hall on the latter evening being more crowded than it has been seen of late. Both entertainments were of the character they were promised to be: there was abundance of fun without the slightest mixture of vulgarity. Mr Liston himself, whichever of his many characters he assumed, was simply irresistible and he left his audiences in entire doubt in which he was most droll. We scarcely like to make a selection, but, if we must, we give the palm to his 'High-tenorant (itinerant) singer,' and 'Johnny,' the 'boy' just returned from the wars. The former was one of the best delineations of the street vocalist we ever saw, and the hornpipe which the latter introduced was not only clever but wonderful. The "make-up," 'Johnny' having suffered a good deal at the hands of the enemy, was admirable, and it was not at all astonishing that it should draw from his 'better half' the exclamation 'Johnny, I hardly knew ye.' Mr Liston was assisted by Mr Montgomery, Miss Rose Clarendon, Miss Etty Gray, and Mr Marsh (accompanist) all of whom acquitted themselves with great credit.[60]

Six months later, Liston was in Dublin with "Johnny" as one of "his most popular songs." *The Ipswich Journal* of March 30, 1872, referred to "Johnny" not as an antiwar tearjerker but as a "Comic Song," and by the end of the year it was being sung in New Zealand.[61]

It was recollected of the humorous Fr. Thomas Burke of Galway (1830–1882), that, apparently in the early 1870s:

One evening he left the room for a moment, and bringing in his niece on his arm—both hastily metamorphosed into ballad-singers, and holding slips torn from an old newspaper—began to sing lustily the 'Galliant [sic] Hussar.' Another evening he stooped his head for a moment behind the piano and rapidly buttoning up the collar of his coat, grasping a stick, and pulling down the skull-cap over his eye, advanced, singing

> With drums and guns, and guns and drums
> The enemy nearly slew ye.
> Oh, darlin' dear, you look so queer,
> 'Faith, Johnny, I hardly knew ye!"[62]

The correspondent for the *Derby Mercury* enjoyed the song's performance during a concert at the Girls' School, which began with "Latour's 'O dolce concento'" by Miss Upton and Miss Whelton. Later in the program came the pure comedy of the mutilated man:

> In the duet, "Och! Johnny I hardly knew ye," no one could have known Johnny, who looked "so queer," with his wooden leg, his relic of an arm, and apology for a nose. Mr (or Miss) Barton, who was equally unrecognisable, complained bitterly of the consequences of "guns and drums," and Mr Pritchard, having lovingly embraced Peggy, confessed that his dancing days were over, and was carried off the stage in his sweetheart's stalwart arms. This fairly brought the house down, and it was some time before the convulsions of laughter had subsided.[63]

The song's perceived hilarity was indeed infectious. In 1874, the *Freeman's Journal* reported the libel trial of Michael Angelo Hayes, a newspaper caricaturist, who had drawn an unkind cartoon portrait of the Dublin City Marshall, John S. Carroll: it depicted Carroll "next a public-house in a conceited and pompous attitude" along with the words, "Johnny, I hardly knew ye." The knowing jury burst immediately into "the most unrestrained laughter." But what, the *Journal* asks rhetorically, had Hayes been getting at? "Johnny, I Hardly Knew Ye" was "a cant phrase, borrowed from a low ribald song.... The subject was that of a soldier running away from a woman and child." The plaintiff's attorney "read some verses of Harry Liston's well-known song," including the words "why did ye skedaddle from me and my [sic] child!" The jury responded with more laughter, and they laughed again when it was pointed out to them that "Johnny" had "returned from the wars with two wooden legs." The jury soon retired and brought back a verdict for the plaintiff, fining Hayes forty pounds in damages. Rather than the horrors of war, the *Journal* clearly understood the song's theme to have been the soldier's unmanly evasion of paternity—and possibly his just deserts. The story was reprinted in several English papers, and Liston was back in Dublin with his most famous song in April, 1879 ("Civic Celebrities"; "Public Notices, April 23, 1879").

"Johnny" even inspired a humorous, personal spin-off by an Irish soldier on campaign, Bernard O'Neill, from Dundalk, a volunteer ambulance-driver for the French army during the Franco-Prussian War. Leeson tells the story, to give "an idea of the poetry which flourished in the Loire districts during the memorable campaigns of 1870–71." Here is the first of five stanzas, and the chorus:

> O'Neill... was able to sing his hardships, and he did so, to the tune of "Johnny, I hardly knew ye." With a few preliminary remarks as to his hoarseness and want of practice in the art of singing, he commenced—
>
> > "On the road to Fontainblew, Hurroo! Hurroo!
> > On the road to Fontainbiew, Hurroo! Hurroo!
> > On the road to Fontaiublew,
> > We war in a h—ll ov a stew,
> > The d—l a knew we knew what to do,
> > Shure all the Prooshans knew ye.
> >
> > Wud me rum an' crumb,
> > An' crumb an' rum,
> > Shure all the boyos knew ye;
> > So Barney, come,
> > Take off yer rum,
> > No matther iv they slew ye."[65]

John Roach's *Johnny I Hardly Knew Ye Irish Comic Songster* (1870), published in New York, is proof that vaudevillians in the United States had not overlooked the song, and the perception of "Johnny, I Hardly Knew Ye" as farce was evidently as widespread in America as elsewhere.[66] One St. Patrick's Day in the early '70s, the "Irish-American veterans" at the Home for Disabled Volunteer Soldiers in Dayton, Ohio, put on a musical revue for a "large number of visitors… from the city, and many from the neighboring cities and towns." Veteran J. C. Gobrecht, who reported on the show, noted that "'Donald Aboo' [sic] by Mr. Larkin, was a most delightful performance." Though "The Rising of the Moon" was sung "with fine effect," and Mr. L. Callahan's performance of "The Irish Brigade" was "rapturously encored," the "vocal gem of the evening" was clearly "Come Where My Love Lies Dreaming," as sung by St. Joseph's Choir. Far more surprising to us, however, may be that an audience of wounded and indigent Civil War veterans in a government home seemed to agree that, in Gobrecht's words, "'Johnny, I hardly Knew You,' as rendered by Mr. L. Callahan in character, was convulsively funny."[67]

By the 1880s, the song seems to have about run its first course of urban popularity, and printed references dwindle away. As late as August 12, 1891, however, an editorial in *The Pall Mall Gazette* (London) alluded to the song offhandedly, and "Johnny" was familiar enough in Australia to be quoted by the prolific novelist Edward Dyson in 1906.[65]

But of greater interest and cultural significance than the song's durability is that not one of the rather numerous early mentions of "Johnny, I Hardly Knew Ye," or reports of its actual singing, treats the song as anything other than boisterous, vulgar, "ribald" farce. Sparling and other editors, of a more refined temperament, perhaps, than Geoghegan, Brereton, Liston, and their intended audiences, occasionally mention an element of "pathos" (presumably found in Peggy's final acceptance of her devastated mate), but no one suggests that the song's intention or import is pacifist, "anti-recruiting," "anti-military," "anti-war," or even serious—or seriously moving—in any way.

One important reason for the audience's light-hearted attitude may be, as noted earlier, that British subjects were not liable to conscription until 1916 during the First World War: the imaginary Johnny had to live with the consequences of his own decision to enlist, and his sweetheart's comic readiness to accept him regardless of his condition undoubtedly resolved any emotional tensions in the music-hall audience. It was, moreover, an enduring stereotype that recruits frequently joined to escape the responsibilities of careless paternity. (As the "Twa Recruiting Sergeants" puts it, "O, laddie, if you've got a sweetheart wi' bairn, /Ye'll easily be rid o' that ill-spun yarn....") If "Johnny" and "Peggy" are destitute, well, that was the necessary condition of the poor, who were expected to accept their lot with dignity. If blind Johnny, with one arm and one leg (or less) was now a "chickenless egg" (a mere shell of a man), who had to be "put in a bowl to beg," that was just grotesque wordplay. When the elderly W. B. Yeats merrily quoted those very words in a literary lecture in 1932, the American poet Marianne Moore writes that her elderly mother, roughly Yeats's age, was notably "amused."[69]

From an Irish nationalist broadside evidently distributed in late 1914 comes a propaganda parody vituperating John Redmond, M. P., leader of the moderate Irish Parliamentary Party and a key proponent of Home Rule. Redmond's sin was in having urged Irishmen of the rival armed militias to join the British Army in the war against the Central Powers:

> You drove them forth to slay the Hun,
> Yes every single mother's son,
> Though a million English slackers run,...
> Och Johnnie I hardly knew you!
>
> You're worse than famine in the land,
> To finish the Gaels you well have planned,
> And leave for the Saxon your native land.
> Och Johnny I hardly knew you![70]

Here may be the first oblique suggestion, nearly fifty years after Geoghegan's song debuted on the variety stage, that it be understood specifically as a protest against the English deployment of Irish recruits in armed conflicts overseas.

That idea was made explicit in 1915 by Lawrence Flick, an American newspaperman, in a fashionably sentimental account of the history and legends of County Tipperary, which suddenly had been made famous by the alleged popularity of "It's a Long Way to Tipperary"—written by Jack Judge in 1912—as a marching song among British troops in France. Flick wrote that the old song of the ruined soldier was more than mere buffoonery; during the period of U.S. neutrality and antiwar sentiment before 1917, Flick thus became the first critic to regard the song as expressing a serious pacifist theme. Flick writes of an "ancient ballad" that

> ...has been sung in Tipperary—and other counties be-sides—at the close of other wars. It isn't a proud marching song to set men's hearts beating high. It embodies rather the wail of the mothers and the wives and the sweethearts when their boys come home from war. And yet it has the touch of humor that all through the centuries of misery in Ireland has kept her people brave and smiling. 'Johnny, I Hardly Knew Ye' is its title, and perhaps some of the 'ould folks' will re-member it.

> > With gun and drum and gun and drum
> > The inimy nearly slew ye,
> > Och, darlin' dear, ye look so queer;
> > Sure, Johnny, I hardly knew ye."

Flick then astutely compares the street ballad from which Geoghegan may have taken inspiration, the one in which the mother addresses her soldier boy in this wise:

> > Oh, were ye drunk, or were ye blind,
> > That ye left the both of your legs behind
> > Or was it walking across the say
> > That ye wore your two shinbones away?

> It is a 'long way from Tipperary' after all that the boys have gone to fight the battles of England....[71]

In November of the same year, 1915, as total World War casualties ap-proached three million, G. Schirmer published Charlotte Milligan Fox's ar-rangements of "Johnny" and "Mistress Magrath" in tandem as *Two Old Irish War-Time Ballads*.

Sinn Féin undoubtedly continued to understand and make use of "Johnny, I Hardly Knew Ye" as an explicit propaganda piece directed toward young

Irishmen who might consider volunteering for the British Army. Ireland, however, was exempted entirely from conscription, which, under provision of the Military Act, came into force for the first time in the United Kingdom on March 2, 1916. Perhaps coincidentally, within a few weeks the song was serving as the basis of a joke printed in an American newspaper, presumably at the expense of the condescending English, though surely this was not its earliest appearance:

PAT'S RETORT

An English tourist was being taken through the country by an Irish jarvey. They were traveling along the road when an ass put its head over the fence and began to bray with all its power. "Well, Pat," said the Englishman. "Is that the 'Wearin' of the Green?'" "Arragh, no, yer honor," said Pat. "That's Johnny I hardly knew you."[72]

The squib reappeared in the *San Jose Mercury Herald* on May 8 and in the *Idaho Daily Statesman* again on Jan. 16, 1918.[73]

By 1918 the use of Patrick Gilmore's stirring melody with various approximations of Joseph Geoghegan's words had already begun to confuse people about what it meant when a band played "When Johnny Comes Marching Home." Almost inevitably there were those in Britain and Ireland who were unfamiliar with Gilmore's words and believed there was only one song:

A man we know remembers his father telling him how the regimental band *greeted them* [emphasis in original] by playing the tune... as they staggered back to base from the front line in Flanders [during World War I]:

Ye haven't an arm and ye haven't a leg,
Ye're an eyeless, chickenless, noseless egg
Ye'll have to be put in a bowl to beg,
Och Johnny, I hardly knew ye...[74]

The British army musicians in the anecdote may have thought they were playing "When Johnny Comes Marching Home," but not all their hearers made that association.

Williams, Graves, and Sparling were among the first critics to endorse the song's literary quality, in its now familiar form, either explicitly or implicitly, and Sparling's text of "Johnny, I Hardly Knew Ye" is one of the few non-Child-ballad folksongs to garner favorable comment outside the field of folk-music research. Yeats influentially included Sparling's words in *A Book of Irish Verse* in 1895 and Yeats's friend, the younger poet and dramatist Padraic Colum, followed suit in *Broadsheet Ballads*.[75]

Much of the song's later international fame was due undoubtedly to the enthusiasm displayed by Yeats and his circle. Colum declared in 1913 that "Johnny" and the far earlier, outlandish description of the "Night before Larry was Stretch'd" (1788) were among the most "characteristic" Irish street ballads.[76] What gave them literary value, he believed, was their expression of the "national temper," namely the "harsh zest in life of people who are below decorum."[77] By thus characterizing the Irish "national temper," Colum was placing a more flattering spin on the loutish stereotypes in both songs, at a time when ethnic stereotyping was usually regarded as the just application of astute observation. But if such songs are in any sense "characteristic," they hardly resemble the general run of Irish street balladry. Colum wrote a one-act play, *The Saxon Shillin'* (1902), specifically to discourage Irishmen from joining the British army, but he seems not to have regarded "Johnny" as a serious adjunct to that effort.

Lady Gregory, Yeats's friend and patron, has the song performed in her "wonder play," *Aristotle's Bellows* (1921), with the variant line, "You're a yellow noseless chickenless egg;" "yellow," perhaps, from jaundice.[78] Yeats's playwright brother, Jack, intended to use "Johnny" as the overture to his play *Apparitions* (1933). In her recent discussion of Jack Yeats's work, Nora A. McGuinness, describes "Johnny" as a "highly ironic antiwar ballad," an "ironic ballad about indifference." Its theme is that "society sends young men off to war and is unmoved when they return unrecognizable and helpless."[79]

The physician, politician, and all-around man of letters Oliver St. John Gogarty, a friend of James Joyce as well as of Yeats, goes further than Padraic Colum in recommending the song: "I have always held that ballad should be Ireland's national anthem," Gogarty wrote in 1937. "It is full of a kind of steadfast courage that can revel in disaster. It is as if the very spirit of Ireland mocked and reveled in vicissitude, deriding Death."[80] (This, of course, appears to be the point of the Clancys' "the enemy never slew ye!") Gogarty reiterated his opinion in the 1950s: "[O]ptimism in the most hopeless circumstances is as Irish as the hero of 'Johnny, I hardly knew you.' In spite of lacking an arm and a leg and one eye Johnny still marches on the road to sweet Athy full of good cheer. It should have been the national anthem: hope in destitution."[81] Indeed, Gogarty was so fond of the song that he once wrote a bombastic send-up of it in sonnet form and Miltonic language to complement the two similar stanzas in "Swinburnese" penned in 1877 by Robert Y. Tyrrell of Trinity College, Dublin.[82] Gogarty—like the Clancy Bros. and Tommy Makem in the early 1960s—saw in Johnny not a heartbreaking victim of war but a wry symbol of Irish indomitability and optimism.

As for Yeats himself, "Johnny, I Hardly Knew Ye" seems to have been one of his favorite songs as well: besides anthologizing it in 1895, and citing it in lectures for decades, he mentions it pointedly in an unintentionally revealing passage in his *Oxford Book of Modern Verse* (1936) in which he defended his antipathy to Wilfred Owen's antiwar poetry:

> If war is necessary, or necessary in our time and place, it is best to forget its suffering.... Florence Farr, returning third-class from Ireland, found herself among Connaught Rangers just returned from the Boer War who described an incident over and over, and always with loud laughter; an unpopular sergeant struck by a shell and turned round and round like a dancer wound in his own entrails. That too may be a right way of seeing war, if war is necessary; the way of the Cockney slums, of Patrick street, of the *Kilmainham Minut*, of *Johnny I hardly knew ye*, of the medieval *Dance of Death*.[83]

The poet Louis MacNeice, raised in Northern Ireland, suggested in 1938 that "Johnny's" popular appeal came partly from its "sardonic criticism of war typical of the hardened cynicism which familiarity with war breeds in ordinary people."[84] Nevertheless, his secondary point is that "the magnificent Irish ballad 'Johnny, I hardly knew ye' is on the face of it just a normally light-hearted ballad on the subject of war." In other words, MacNeice had to look beneath the surface in a way that today may seem unnecessary, to find anything that was not "light-hearted."

Several years after the end of World War II, the American poet Babette Deutsch found in the song a "gay brutality" along with a certain "raw truth," and Horace Reynolds of Harvard found an opportunity to praise the song's "desperate gaiety."[85]

However they are qualified, these poetic and critical evaluations make it plain that one reason for the canonization of "Johnny" among "Irish ballads" was its rarely acknowledged ability to stimulate pure ghoulish glee with no particular bearing on war, conscience, or any similar concern. That ability, rather than compassion for the victims of war, seems to be precisely the quality that most nineteenth-century audiences exhibited, appreciated, and understood.

W.H. Auden's *Oxford Book of Light Verse* (1941) included the lyrics once again, as did Frank O'Connor's *Book of Ireland* (1959). Dalton Trumbo's novel *Johnny Got his Gun*, the well-known antiwar nightmare about a doughboy dismembered as completely as Geoghegan's Johnny, was published two days after the German attack on Poland. The *Saturday Review* called it "The most shocking novel about the horrors of war ever written!"[86] What had been little more than amusing farce to one era had become terrible tragedy to the next.

First no more than a comic song, then a striking set of anthologized verses, "Johnny, I Hardly Knew Ye" was recorded commercially at least twice during the 1920s: by Shaun O'Nolan, with the romantic "Enniskillen Dragoon" on the flip side, and by Dan Sullivan's Shamrock Band (vocals by Murty Rabbett.)[87] Three stanzas and the chorus appeared in the left-oriented *People's Songs Bulletin* (forerunner of *Sing Out!*) for February, 1949. Described as "beautiful... piercing and poignant," the verses are said to date "from the 18th century when Ireland's youth was drafted wholesale [sic] to fight England's wars throughout the globe." The song "was recently rediscovered by Betty Sanders, who has made a beautiful recording of it, available through Alco Distributors.... When you sing it, take it easy and mean every word you sing."[88]

Vienna-born Martha Schlamme's 1952 and 1954 recordings, with the addition of Les Pine's vow that "They'll never take our sons again!" reinvented the song as a militant, anti-draft, antiwar protest. The version sung by the Irish poet and playwright Patrick Galvin on his album of *Irish Street Songs* (1956) is said to be "from Galway," and thus lacks the American anti-draft stanza. Ending with a series of plaintive hurroos, Galvin's measured delivery, to an astringent banjo accompaniment by Al Jeffery, lends plausibility to the accompanying note, which might have been thought fantastic ninety years earlier: "This is undoubtedly one of the most powerful of all antiwar laments." He remarks that, though the song is "known all over Ireland," it is "not very often sung."[89] In abridged versions like Galvin's, the derisive comedy vanishes, and only the surreal horror is left behind. D. K. Wilgus, in a review for a folklore journal, praised the "sardonic savagery" of Galvin's song; a kind of which "the American 'When Johnny Comes Marching Home' is a not-even-pale copy."[90] Cynthia Gooding recorded the song in 1958, as did a deeply overwrought Glenn Yarborough, who sighs in anguish as a harmonica adds blue notes to his pop-sounding rendition on *Here We Go, Baby* (1958).[91] Perhaps better than anyone, the Clancy Bros. & Tommy Makem bring out the song's strange mixture of qualities. In their modern and refined version, the song generates poignantly complicated feelings: it is alternately comic, macabre, pathetic, and defiant, its implications not quite diluted by its grotesquerie: "cruel, but somehow satisfying," according to the novelist Emma Donoghue.[92]

One of the more significant lyrical changes appended to the song since Pine's anti-draft stanza of about 1950 appears to be the responsibility of the Irish writer Dominic Behan, who offers six stanzas "arranged and adapted" by himself, and copyright 1965. All of these are familiar but for the last, which seems to gloat sarcastically that defeat, mutilation, humiliation, ridicule, and scorn are the soldier's deserved fate:

> "But yeh'll never go to war again haroo haroo,
> "Against much better fighting men haroo,
> "For they showed yeh how to run me boy
> the whole way home to sweet Athy,
> "Oh darlin'! Did yeh come home to die?
> Johnny I hardly knew yeh.[93]

Behan's words skate over the inconveniences of conquest by those same enemy forces, the "much better fighting men," who apparently should not have been resisted in the first place. Behan's stanza, like Makem's comparably inapt "never slew ye!" remains unique.

Screen star and soprano Maureen O'Hara recorded "Johnny" in a sensitive, orchestrally supported performance on *Her Favorite Irish Songs* (1962).[94] A half century on, Amazon.com listed nearly a hundred distinct, downloadable recordings, ranging in style from the hearty theatricality of Makem and the Clancys, to the headbanging "Celtic punk" of the Dropkick Murphys, to the ethereality of choral groups like the Robert Shaw Chorale (1968) and the West Coast Mennonite Chamber Choir (2003), to Joan Baez accompanying herself on guitar in the 1970s—with brooding, interstanzaic "mmmms" to underscore the tragedy of the tale.[95]

In-between approaches include backup with fifes and drums, banjos and drums, guitars and drums, everything but drums and guns. Singers' accents run from Irish to Californian to bad-fake Irish. Recent recordings sometimes include a bit of contemporary rewriting, sometimes to increase the erotic tenderness of the damsel's feelings. (Though "damsel," in the context of the skit described by the *Derby Mercury* of 1879, was undoubtedly intended as an additional touch of irony). Janis Ian has her damsel inquire, with castrational undertones,

> "Where are your arms that held me tight?
> When first you went to join the fight
> And we'll *never, no more*, share the night!"[96]

> The rock group Easterhouse (*Contenders*, 2001) rewrites the song to include nationalist lines like

> With guns and drums to Wexford town
> Hero! Hero!…
> With guns and drums to Wexford town,
> The English lords did rule ya!…[97]

Folk-rock performances are generally frenetic, while many solo vocalists exploit the melodrama of varying *accelerandi* and *decelerandi*. Steeleye Span took ideas from the song for its antiwar pastiche, "Fighting for Strangers" (1976). Soprano Ailish Tynan and pianist Iain Burnside do classical justice to Herbert Hughes's own arrangement on *A Purse of Gold: Irish Songs by Herbert Hughes* (2007), and the popular mezzo-soprano Ann Murray and pianist Graham Johnson do likewise on Irish Songs (2009). On *Piratically Incorrect* (2008), the Musical Blades—exemplars of the post-*Pirates of the Caribbean* (2003) "pirate band" phenomenon—present another brand-new text about pirates battling with "guns and rum and rum and guns."[98]

Then there are the YouTube performances. As of July, 2011, YouTube offered about two dozen amateur and professional videos from as far afield as Poland, France, and Germany. The public responses often either stress the song's "beauty" or denounce it as pacifist propaganda. A 2008 upload of the Chad Mitchell Trio's deft antiwar composite of the two "Johnnies" (1961), skillfully illustrated by the poster with alternating clips of international wartime triumphs and agonies, received over one hundred comments, many of them quite emotional.[99] YouTube postings of separate recordings of both songs, in various styles, elicited similarly fervid comments from the YouTube community. Despite drastic changes in the song's interpretation, it would be a mistake to conclude from the transformation of "Johnny, I Hardly Knew Ye" from a comic song into a bitter commentary on war that average Victorians were any more callous towards human suffering than people today (though some might argue from other evidence that indeed they were). Two fundamental elements seem to have changed: the first is simply the style of artistic expression. Bitter irony (to be distinguished from the cleverly satirical Swiftian kind) as an aesthetic idiom has burgeoned in the arts only in the twentieth century: Marcel Duchamp's celebrated display, in 1913, of a common urinal as a work of art titled "Fountain" led the way toward an increased expectation (though only among sophisticates) that any artistic production might well be intended ironically, and by the end of the 1960s savage irony had become a common tactic in literary and musical treatments of war: the film of Joan Littlewood's *Oh What a Lovely War!* (1969) is a prime example. But a clear proof to the Victorians that "Johnny" was meant as no more than outrageous humor was their shared expectation for tragedy to be fully developed, sentimental, solemn, and melodramatic. On the cover of a song of tragedy, one would expect to see a conventional gesture of horror and despair, such as a lowered head with a

forearm thrown over the eyes, not the neatly dressed damsel's conventional "gesture of surprise" noted by Hughes. Examples exist in profusion, on
all kinds of subjects, but one thinks right away of the truly maudlin and
successful popular songs and poems of the American Civil War: "Just Before the Battle, Mother," "The Drummer Boy of Shiloh," "The Last Fierce
Charge," "The Dying Volunteer," "Mother, Is the Battle Over?" "Weeping
Sad and Lonely," "The Vacant Chair," "Brother's Fainting at the Door," and
many more. "Write a Letter to My Mother" (1864) shows how patently
contrived situations were thought to be extremely moving and cathartic:

> Raise me in your arms, my brother.
> Let me see the glorious sun.
> I am weary, faint and dying,
> How is the battle, lost or won?
>
> Write a letter to my mother,
> Send it when her boy is dead.
> That he perish'd by his brother,
> Not a word of that be said.[100]

Eleanor C. Donnelly's poem, "More Nurses" (1864), sets forth the Victorian conception of the meaning of wounds and death in battle, a conception
rarely questioned before the First World War:

> These wounds are more precious than ghastly,
> Fame presses her lip to each scar,
> While she chants of that glory which vastly
> Transcends all the horrors of war.
>
> …
>
> Touch him gently; most sacred the duty
> Of dressing that poor, shattered hand!
> God spare him to rise in his beauty,
> And battle once more for his land![101]

In Ireland, perhaps the most apposite example of the genre, though without Donnelly's spirituality, is the nationalist Charles J. Kickham's "Glen of Aherlow" or "Patrick Sheehan" (1857), whose versified tale of disaster is calculated to wring tears from a stone—or at least from a stone with any imagination:

...My father died; I closed his eyes,
...outside our cabin door;
The landlord and the sheriff too, were there
...the day before!
And then my loving mother, and sisters
...three also,
Were forced to go with broken hearts,
...from the Glen of Aherlow

For three long months, in search of work, I wandered
...far and near;
I went then to the poorhouse to see my mother dear;
The news I heard nigh broke my heart; but
...still, in all my woe,
I blessed the friends who made their graves
...in the Glen of Aherlow.

Bereft of home and kith and kin, with plenty all around,
I starved within my cabin, and slept upon the ground;
But cruel as my lot was, I ne'er did hardship know
Till I joined the English army, far away from Aherlow.

"Rouse up there," says the Corporal, "You lazy
...Hirish 'ound;
Why don't you hear, you sleepy dog, the call
...'to arms' sound?"
Alas, I had been dreaming of days long, long ago;
I woke before Sebastopol, and not in Aherlow

I groped to find my musket—how dark I thought
...the night!
O blessed God, it was not dark, it was the
...broad daylight!
And when I found that I was blind, my tears
...began to flow;
I longed for even a pauper's grave in the Glen of
...Aherlow[102]

For Irish ballad audiences, *there* was an antiwar song, an anti-recruiting song, and an anti-English song to boot. It could still be heard sung in Co. Fermanagh, Ulster, a century and a quarter after Kickham wrote it (Glassie 455).

Compared to Kickham's Patrick Sheehan, crushed and crushed again by terrible misfortune, the characters of "Johnny, I Hardly Knew Ye" are blatant caricatures, puppets put on stage to entertain us with their horribly painful and insoluble plight. Stage-Irish accents were recognized as an automatic signal for laughter, like the black English of the minstrel shows, and "Peggy's" way with words in nineteen-century versions is ludicrously expressive. "Real people," one hears the Victorians say, "simply don't speak or act like that." Nineteenth-century ethnic prejudice was ubiquitous, and the Irish on stage were generally expected to be hilarious, impoverished drunkards. Even in 1911, in his investigation of the sources of humor, the ordinarily humane philosopher Henri Bergson asked innocently, "Why does one laugh at a negro?" He wasn't sure—perhaps, he thought, black people seemed to be white people covered absurdly with soot—but evidently Bergson's generation expected that kind of laughter to be the norm. An Englishman might have wondered, similarly, "Why do we laugh at the Irish?" His answer might have been, "Because they seem to be English, but their accents are absurd and they act like clowns."

Many Victorians, including Bernard O'Neill, must have realized as well that no soldier would be likely to survive Johnny's multiple wounds and amputations on an 1860s battlefield, in an age when medical science had not yet developed antibiotics or anti-tetanus or knew that surgical instruments had to be sterilized. The sick "humor" of the situation is comparable to that displayed nowadays in Matt Groening's "Itchy & Scratchy" cartoons, which feature a cat whose only function is to be tortured and gruesomely dismembered by gleeful, sadistic mice. Farcical skits like Harry Liston's (and L. Callahan's) with broad physical comedy and outlandish makeup, were the closest thing the world had to the impossible humor of animated cartoons. British wars of the nineteenth century were small, far away, and fought by faceless, self-exiled men for whom the general public (as in Kipling's "Tommy") had little sympathy. The situation imagined by Geoghegan was far more an idle exercise in sadistic humor than a heartfelt protest against war.

There remains the popular assumption that bandmaster Patrick Gilmore transformed a realistic, bitterly "antiwar" Johnny into a triumphalist, enthusiastically "pro-war" Johnny. Why has that groundless fantasy become accepted wisdom? Partly it was because the primacy of "Johnny, I Hardly Knew Ye" was blandly asserted by both Herbert Hughes and Alan Lomax. But I believe it is chiefly because it fits into a simple narrative of decent humanity ceaselessly victimized by the "establishment," the "system," that goes on to profit from human suffering, while other, more oblivious, victims cheer it on.

In this populist view, which is restricted to neither the right nor the left, the "people," the "folk" (in this case specifically the long-sentimentalized Irish), have always recognized war's horror and futility; they dare to decry it in a song sung "underground" for generations and based on a cruel and needless war that is carefully unmentioned in "official" school histories. An American army officer annexes the tune and cynically recasts the situation—a devastated soldier's return to abject poverty—into a cheery triumph with pealing church bells and public spectacle. Gilmore's lyrics, however, are hardly "pro-war": they are explicitly "pro" homecoming and public gratitude. Yet their celebratory mood allows reinterpretation of the song as an attempt to suppress everything deep and truthful in the supposed "Irish original."

From this perspective, the enormous popularity of Gilmore's song as a patriotic staple makes the presumed "substitution" all the more galling, as the controlling establishment wins again. Surely that point of view was in part behind the popularity of "Johnny, I Hardly Knew Ye" among progressive and frankly leftist singers of folksongs in the post-Kennedy 1960s and '70s, the era of the Vietnam War. One twin—Johnny-thevictim—was mustered to drive out the other—Johnny-the-victor.

The Victorian and twentieth-century writers who alluded in print to "Johnny, I Hardly Knew Ye" have left a body of critical response that is unusual for any folksong short of "Edward" and "Sir Patrick Spens." A current consensus also exists. The lowbrow comedy of 1867 was highbrow commentary a hundred years later. Like Benjamin Luxon, singers are not usually prepared to explain clearly just what appeals to them in a song beyond its music or overall "feeling."

This is hardly surprising. Few people wish to examine their own tastes, and it is difficult to put personal feelings about any work of art into words. Even so, "Johnny, I Hardly Knew Ye" is occasionally commented on in cyberspace, and what its more articulate singers and hearers have to say about it is worthy of attention. General characterizations include *awesome, beautiful, freaking amazing, stark and realistic, grisly* and *gruesome*. Of course, the manner of performance is at least as important as the lyrics; but by the same token, no modern singers seem to see in "Johnny" any sort of joke, no matter how it might be presented. Indeed, one suspects that a misguided attempt to play it as humor after the wars of the past century would be booed off any civilized stage.

The Internet quotations that follow come from a website for fans of traditional, folklike, and singer-songwriter music, in the decade between 1997 and 2007. It took one, quite atypical, writer many years to feel sure of aspects of the song that the Victorians had apparently found obvious; yet there is still no hint that he finds the song "funny":

> [T]he song makes perfect sense if you understand that the girl singing is simply delighted at what's happened to this fellow who got her pregnant and then ran off to the army. She's gloating and rubbing it in… [Her] tactlessness used to bother me in the 60's, when I was trying to hear it as anti-war. No matter how sadly and lovingly they sang it, the inappropriate words came through. Then, one day, I thought about that running away or skeedaddling or whatever, and it came to me what he did and what she thought of it.

Another writer detects humor, but not of the boisterous 1870s kind:

> I like it better sung with "the army nearly slew ye" rather than "the enemy"—because it's joining the army led to all this…. I think she's talking realistically and stoically…. Facing up to the future with a touch of bitter humour.

This comment seems to project more sensitivity into the song than was ever there:

> A wonderful song about what disability means to family members.

Another writer, whose text has "Where are your eyes that *used to smile?*" like the "Irish eyes" in a later, even more famous song, makes the song's admonitory function explicit, though it seems to be directed chiefly toward the secondary victim:

> It depicts a deeply personal tragedy in one family…. It brings it home, and says, "This could be *you*" when you first see your soldier returned from the wars.

Some singers know exactly what they want to do to an audience:

> You can… do a really killing version of 'Johnny, I hardly knew you..' Goes like this:

> Start by singing 'When Johnny comes marching home' slowly… ending with:

> > When Johnny comes marching home again,
> > Hurrah, hurrah
> > Who'll give him a hearty welcome then,
> > hurrah, hurrah,
> > WITH ONE GOOD LEG AND ONE EYE GONE AND BLOODSTAINS ON HIS UNIFORM

Will we all be glad when Johnny comes marching home?

Work up a good head of anger… and you should finish up
with someone in tears![103]

An English YouTube subscriber who posted Janis Ian's version accompanied by gruesome images sums up the modern view of the song's import
in a post to the online *Janis Ian Forum*: "the mutilation of human beings
and destruction of human life in military action is sickening and obscene,
but I think that's… the point that the song makes. The question is, should
we or should we not confront people with the reality of what guns and
bombs do and ask them to think about it?"[104]

Under the title of "When Johnny Comes Marching Home," dulcimer
instructors Bud and Donna Ford complete Gilmore's opening stanza with:

You haven't an arm, you haven't a leg,
You'll have to put with a bowl to beg.
And we'll all feel gay when
Johnny comes marching home.

Johnny won't march and Johnny won't cheer, hurrah, hurrah,
Oh Johnny for you we shed a tear, hurrah, hurrah,
Our cheers are empty, our tears are dry,
We sent too many young men to die.
And will you feel gay
When Johnny comes marching home?[105]

"Our favorite," the Fords note. "Quite a reversal of the usual triumphant
version, it portrays the grim, stark reality of war. Not glamour, but pain and
bitterness at the aftermath of violence." And sarcasm for the presumably
complacent audience as well, who are fancied as feeling "gay" at the sight
of Johnny's condition. A minority of singers imagine the usually unnamed
woman to be a "widow," with Johnny as her son.[106]

One text poeticizes the refrains into "O rue! O rue!" and imagines the returned Johnny as "mindless" as well as boneless. Poeticizing may also account for the occasional variant title, "Johnny, I Hardly Knew Thee."

When at a 2006 rally in New York City, the actor and Green-Party candidate Malachy McCourt sang three-stanzas angrily and unaccompanied, with quietly consoling "hurroos," he stressed the song's current political relevance:

> This… is the first time in the history of the United States that the government has been seized by thieves, thugs, terrorists, evangelical murderers, holy hypocrites, and despots. [Applause]… And our troops, our soldiers, are fighting in a far-distant land for the right of our government to take away our freedoms. A very ironic thing that is, you see. [Applause.]… And now… everybody is going against the war.… And always, in every movement, there must be always music, and here's the best antiwar song ever written:
>
>> Whilst going the road to sweet Athy…
>> A stick in my hand and a tear in me eye,
>> A doleful damsel I heard cry,
>> "Johnny, I hardly knew ye!"
>>
>> "With your guns and drums and drums and guns…
>>
>> "Ye haven't an arm, ye haven't a leg…
>> Ye're an eyeless, chickenless, boneless egg,
>> Ye'll soon be put with a bowl to beg
>> Johnny, I hardly knew ye!"
>>
>> "With your guns and drums and drums and guns…
>> "They'll never take our boys again, hurroo, hurroo…

They'll never take our boys again
To turn them into fighting men,
Johnny, I swear it to ye!"[107]

Though Federal law requires young men in the United States to register for a possible draft in case of a national emergency, American conscription has been suspended since 1973, making the final stanza something of an anachronism unless, as is likely, it urges parents to keep their children out of the armed forces. McCourt's humanism, however, sentimentally overlooks the fact that most members of a volunteer military *want to be* "fighting men" (and women). He did not mention the song's title, but the summary of the event identifies it as "When Johnny Comes Marching Home." This is the title by which many people now know it, with Gilmore's innocent (or suspect) verses, ending with a plain endorsement of "love and friendship," increasingly forgotten. (I myself heard Gilmore's title applied to Geoghegan's song as long ago as 1971.)

When McCourt sang "Johnny" again at a later peace demonstration, one grandmother found it so "heartbreaking" that she stood "mesmerized and moved to tears:"

> I think if Bush could hear Malachy McCourt sing that deeply affecting ballad, it might turn even *his* indifferent heart around and he'd stop murdering our young military. The lyrics may be the most moving ones of all in the anti-war song repertoire and go right to the core of the tragedy of war.[108]

"Johnny, I Hardly Knew Ye" is finally one of the very few traditional songs out of thousands that still enjoys an authentically regenerating "folk" existence. Though strongly influenced by professionally introduced, commercial versions, the various changes in length, wording, tone, and emphasis are precisely the kinds of change seen in the most rigorously defined traditional songs of any period. "Johnny, I Hardly Knew Ye," however, gains in interest from its jarring parodic marriage to the tune of a parallel song having an antithetically optimistic theme. This incongruity between the "frame" (the vigorous tune and the cheerful associations of Gilmore's song) and the "picture" (the stark verbal content) may once have been perceived as an element of humor: now it is thought to be—by those who notice it—artistic, tragic commentary. (It is probable, however, that fewer young people than ever have any familiarity with Gilmore's song, particularly its lyrics, partly because what once seemed thoroughly harmless is now sometimes seen as subtly encouraging support for the military-industrial complex.)

The appropriation of the more familiar American tune for the mock-Irish song may have been inevitable; even Gilmore's title recommends it as a good match. "Johnny, I Hardly Knew Ye," moreover, turned from a song of "Irish wit and humor" into a "message song" denouncing militarism partly through intentional changes to the words themselves since the early 1950s, but more fundamentally, as a result of the unprecedented, sensibility-altering public experience—and vivid reporting and cinematic images—of the First and Second World Wars, the Cold War, and the corresponding increase in the public's feelings of concern for its wounded veterans and their families. It has been refashioned and reinterpreted to carry a new meaning for a new world.[105]

From the chance mixture of nineteenth-century grotesquerie and the increasingly horrific nature of twentieth-century warfare, current texts of "Johnny I Hardly Knew Ye" distill a draught of grief and horror and a consequent, often strident, message of eternal pacifism. Patrick S. Gilmore's song was a promise: fortunate Johnny will come marching home to a hero's welcome, and after suitable festivities, everyone may be expected to lead lives of contentment and peace. Current redactions of J. B. Geoghegan's song, however, are a warning: Johnny will limp home helpless, dehumanized, devastated, and mute, and no one concerned will be happy again. That includes the audience, particularly when Johnny's fate is laid at its own doorstep. The conventionally upbeat lyrics of "When Johnny Comes Marching Home" have been condemned as propaganda, but current versions of the newly propagandistic "Johnny, I Hardly I Knew Ye" are believed to tell the essential truth about war. In a world beyond Gilmore's and Geoghegan's imagining, where civilians are often more likely to become war casualties than soldiers, each song has come to carry a social significance that would have amazed its author.[110]

Notes

1. *Luxon: Johnny I hardly knew'ya* [sic]. YouTube: <http://www.youtube.com/watch?v=NCfuar4sAKY>. Accessed July 10, 2011.

2. *The Clancy Bros. & Tommy Makem.* Sound rec. N.Y.: Tradition TLP-1042, 1961.

3. *Johnny, I Hardly Knew Ye – Clancy Brothers & Tommy Makem.* YouTube: <http://www.youtube.com/watch?v=4VoOovy0ZNs>. Accessed July 10, 2011.

4. Makem's son writes that his father believed "Johnny" to have been "JFK's favorite song" (John F. Kennedy, of course, had been seriously injured in the Pacific during the Second World War). Conor Makem, "First Person by Conor Makem" <http://www.fosters.com/apps/pbcs.dll/article?AID=/2011 0120/GJNEWS_01/701209783>. Accessed July 9, 2011.

5. Alan Lomax, ed., *The Folk Songs of North America in the English Language* (Garden City, N.Y.: Doubleday, 1960), p. 84; Penny Perrick, "Athy's the Limit," *Sunday Times* (London), Dec. 13, 1992, p. 11; Library of Congress, *Performing Arts Encyclopedia.* <http://lcweb2.loc.gov/diglib/ihas/loc.natlib.ihas.200000024/default.html>. Accessed July 10, 2011.

6. Robert V. Wells, *Life Flows on in Endless Song: Folksongs and American History* (Cambridge: Cambridge Univerity Press, 2009), p. 63.

7. [Patrick S. Gilmore], *When Johnny Comes Marching Home*, by Louis Lambert (Boston: H. Tolman & Co., 1863).

8. Wendy Doniger, *The Implied Spider: Politics and Theology in Myth* (N.Y.: Columbia University Press, 2010), p. 115.

9. Wells, *Life Flows on in Endless Song*, pp. 63–64.

10. "Johnny, I Hardly Knew Ye," *Sing Out!* (Oct., 1951), p. 16.

11. *Henry's Songbook: Johnny, I Hardly Knew Ye.* <http://mysongbook.de/msb/songs/j/johnnyih.html>. Accessed Jan. 25, 2004.

12. H. Halliday Sparling, ed., *Irish Minstrelsy* [Second ed.] (London: Walter Scott, 1888), p. 512.

13. Henry Marshall, *Ceylon: A General Description of the Island and its Inhabitants* (London: William H. Allen, 1846), *passim*; Peter C. Luebke, "Battle of Seven Pines–Fair Oaks," *Encyclopedia Virginia*. Brendan Wolfe, ed., Virginia Foundation for the Humanities. 12 Apr. 2011 <http://www.EncyclopediaVirginia.org/Seven_Pines_Battle_of>. Accessed July 30, 2011.

14. Sparling, *Irish Minstrelsy*, pp. 350–352.

15. James Joyce, *A Portrait of the Artist as a Young Man* (N.Y.: Huebsch, 1916), p. 24. Despite the imperfect rhyme, some American singers now pronounce it as "Athee."

16. Alfred M. Williams, ed., *The Poets and Poetry of Ireland* (Boston: James Osgood, 1881), p. 180.

17. Francis O'Neill, ed., *O'Neill's Music of Ireland* (Chicago: Lyon & Healey, 1903), p. 82 and unpaged index; Francis O'Neill, ed., *Waifs and Strays of Gaelic Melody* (Chicago: Lyon & Healey, 1922), p. 52.

18. Charlotte Milligan Fox, *Two Old Irish War-Time Ballads* (N.Y.: G. Schirmer, 1915); Colm O Lochlainn, ed., *Irish Street Ballads* (N.Y.: Corinth Books, 1960), pp. 142–143. Pitt of Seven Dials printed an early version of "Mrs. McGrath" under the title of "Teddy O'Gra" "between 1819 and 1844" according to the Bodleian: Harding B 11(3746), which also includes the lines quoted.

19. Herbert Hughes, ed., *Irish Country Songs*. 3 vols. (London: Boosey & Co., 1909, 1915, 1934), III, pp. iv–v.

20. Harold E. Raugh, *The Victorians at War, 1815–1914* (Santa Barbara, Calif.: ABC-CLIO, 2004), p. 22.

21. Hughes, *Irish Country Songs*, p. v.

22. Frederic Boase, *Modern English Biography*. 2 vols. (Truro: Netherton & Worth, 1892), s.v. *Geoghegan*.

23. "Gilmore the Great," *Irish World and American Industrial Liberator* (New York City) Sept. 3, 1892, n.p.

24. Frank J. Cipolla, "Patrick S. Gilmore: The Boston Years," *American Music* 6 (Autumn, 1988), pp. 281–292.

25. Charles Nelson Kent, *History of the Seventeenth Regiment New Hampshire Volunteer Infantry, 1862–1863* (Concord, N.H.: pvtly. ptd., 1898), p. 212.

26. Lomax, *Folk Songs*, p. 84.

27. James R. Fuld, *The Book of World-Famous Music*, Fifth ed. (N.Y.: Dover, 2000), p. 523.

28. Fuld, *Book of World-Famous Music*, p. 524.

29. *Johnny Fill Up the Bowl*, arr. by J. Durnal (N.Y.: John J. Daly, 1863). [Repository copy: U. S. Library of Congress, shelf-mark M 1640.D.]

30. Raymond Monelle, *The Sense of Music* (Princeton, N.J.: Princeton U. P., 2000), p. 79; Fuld, *Book of World-Famous Music*, p. 524.

31. Fuld, *Book of World-Famous Music*, p. 524.

32. James F. Leisy, ed., *The Folksong Abecedary* (N.Y.: Hawthorn, 1966), p. 195.

33. Frank Kidson, *Traditional Tunes* (Oxford: C. Taphouse & Son, 1891), p. 17.

34. Elizabeth Duane Gillespie, *A Book of Remembrance* (Philadelphia: J. B. Lippincott, 1901), p. 78.

35. Ronnie Clark, personal communication, incl. mp3 of Arthur Lochhead, August 8, 2011; Norman Buchan & Peter Hall, eds., *The Scottish Folksinger* (Glasgow: Collins, 1978), p. 41.

36. Kent, *History of the Seventeenth Regiment*, p. 212.

37. W. A. Linn, "A Critical Criticism," *Yale Literary Magazine* 33 (Oct., 1867), pp. 25–30.

38. *Songs Compiled for Use of Minnesota Commandery, Military Order of the Loyal Legion of the United States* (St. Paul, Minn.: Pioneer Press, 1886), pp. 65–66.

39. George Lyman Kittredge, "The Three Ravens in Ohio," *Journal of American Folk-Lore* 31 (1918), p. 275.

40. [Arlo Bates; A.T. Parker; & J. E. Chapman, eds.], *Songs of Bowdoin* (Boston: J. Frank Giles, 1875), p 39.

41. Norman Cazden, Herbert Haufrecht, & Norman Studer, *Folk Songs of the Catskills* (Albany, N.Y.: SUNY Press 1982), raise documentary questions that should be disposed of here. By confusing the Daly-Durnal "Johnny Fill Up the Bowl" with a satire called "For Bales" published in New Orleans in 1864 (with an identical "fill up the bowl" chorus), the editors dispute Fuld's dating of the former and reassert the primacy of Gilmore's song. The editors then state confidently (p. 368) that despite its September, 1863, copyright date,

> the words of 'When Johnny Comes Marching Home' were surely in print, though without attribution, in 1861. They are to be seen in two songsters published that year, *Charlie Monroe's Clown Song Book* and *Dr. J. L. Thayer's Clown Song Book*, both issued in Philadelphia by R. F. Simpson.

Anonymous publication of the lyrics in 1861 might cast doubt on Gilmore's claim to even the words of his most famous creation. Cazden, Haufrecht, and Studer, however, are doubtless mistaken. According to WorldCat Online, *Charley* [sic] *Monroe's Clown Song Book* was not published till 1867; Thayer's publication is untraceable under that title, though *Dr. J. L. Thayer's Laugh and Grow Fat* dime song book is advertised in 1878. The most likely explanation for the seemingly "early" dates may be no more than a librarian's cataloguing note. For cataloguing purposes, libraries have given many undated Civil War-era songsters tentative dates of "1861?" or "1861–?" Extensive digital searches reveal no indication that the song "When Johnny Comes Marching Home" existed before 1863.

The editors state also that Bronson records traditional examples of "The Twa Sisters" (Child 10) set to variants of the "Johnny" tune. This too is in error: while the tunes share the *stanzaic form*, their *shapes* do not much resemble that of "Johnny."

Ranch-hand Stan Jones turned the famous melody into 4/4 for his hit song "Ghost Riders in the Sky" (1949). Jones' song is now sometimes assumed popularly to be an example of nineteenth-century American folklore.

42. Peter Linebaugh, *The London Hanged: Crime and Civil Society in the Eighteenth Century* (London: Verso, 2003), p. 300.

43. Alfred Perceval Graves, ed., *Songs of Irish Wit and Humour* (London: Chatto & Windus, 1884), pp. 151–153.

44. Alfred M. Williams, *Poets and Poetry*, p. 180.

45. J. B. Geoghegan, *Johnny, I Hardly Know Ye* (London: Metzler, 1867).

46. *Johney I Hardly Knew Ye* (Dublin: P. Brereton, printer, n. d. [ca 1867]). [Bodleian Ballads Catalogue Harding B26 (297).]

47. Gale Huntington, ed., *Songs the Whalemen Sang* (Barre, Mass.: Barre, 1964), pp 120–122.

48. *Johnny, I Hardly Knew Ye* (Manchester: T. Pearson, n.d.).

49. [Gilmore], *When Johnny Comes Marching Home*, p. 2.

50. "Public Amusements." *Caledonian Mercury* (Jan. 21, 1865), n. p.

51. "The Christy's Minstrels in Bold-street," *The Era* (London)(May 7, 1865), n.p.

52. George Christy & Charles White, *Christy's and White's Ethiopian Melodies* (Philadelphia: T. B. Peterson & Bros., 1854), p. 37.

53. Some further examples, including an antedating:

"I got beside him—shouted out hurroo! / And when I wav'd my hand, he wav'd his too!" (*The Dublin Mail; or, Intercepted Correspondence* [N.Y.: H. I. Megarey, 1822], p. 122.)

"Then, springing upon the formidable persecutor, he wrenched the weapon from his hand, and flung it into the air.

"'Hooroo!' shouted Jemmy, dancing with passion, and reiterating the wild exultant cry so frequently heard in an Irish *scrimmidge* [sic]."

(Benson E. Hill, "The Irishman in Egypt," *New Monthly Magazine and Humorist* [1837, Pt. I], p. 277.)

"At night, O how silly along Piccadilly I wandered, when up came a beautiful dame—Hurroo, says the lady, how do you do, Paddy? Says I, pretty well, ma'am, I hope you're the same." (James Smith, *Memoirs, Letters and Comic Miscellanies in prose and verse of the late James Smith, Esq.* Ed. H. Smith [London: Henry Colburn, 1840], p. 301.)

"Those nearest the door hammered it with sticks and fists, and yelled for it to be opened. "Hurroo!" they cried. "God save Irelan'! Hurroo! hurroo!"—Wait! Whisht! What's that? Begob, it's Micky! Hurroo for Independence! Hurroo for Micky! *Boo! Boo! Hurroo I Boo!* Micky for iver! Three cheers for Micky! *Boo! Boo!*" (Shan F. Bullock, *The Awkward Squads and Other Stories* [London: Cassell, 1893], p. 238.

54. "Fashion and Varieties," *Freeman's Journal and Daily Commercial Advertiser* (Dublin) (July 6, 1867).

55. Advertisement, *Freeman's Journal and Daily Commercial Advertiser* (Dublin) (September 2, 1867).

56. "General Domestic News," *Hampshire Telegraph and Sussex Chronicle* (Portsmouth, England), September 7, 1867.

57. "Ecclesiastical Intelligence," *Newcastle Courant* (September 13, 1867).

58. *Bird of the Wilderness.* Broadsheet. Glasgow: Poet's Box, 1868. <http://digital.nls.uk/broadsides/broadside.cfm/id/16289/criteria/%22hardly%20knew%20ye%22>. Accessed June 12, 2011

59. Cazden, Haufrecht, & Studer, *Catskills*, p. 368.

60. "Local and District," *North Wales Chronicle* (Bangor) (September 4, 1869).

61. "Public Notices," *Freeman's Journal and Daily Commercial Advertiser* (Dublin) (April 11, 1870); "Foresters' Annual Soiree," *The Ipswich Journal* (March 30, 1872); "Loyal Blue Spur Lodge," *Tuapeka* [N.Z.] *Times* (Apr. 18, 1872), p. 7 <http://paperspast.natlib.govt.nz/cgibin/paperspast?a=d&d=TT18720418.2.29>. Accessed July 11, 2011.

62. William J. Fitzpatrick, *The Life of the Very Rev. Thomas N. Burke, O.P.* Vol. 2. (London: Kegan, Paul, Trench, 1885), p. 175.

63. "District News, Rolleston," *Derby* [Eng.] *Mercury* (Feb. 26, 1879).

64. "The Civic Celebrities," *Freeman's Journal and Daily Commercial Advertiser* (Dublin) (June 15, 1874); "Public Notices," *Freeman's Journal and Daily Commercial Advertiser* (April 11, 1870).

65. Michael Leeson, *Reminiscences of the Franco-Irish Ambulance* (Dublin: M'Glashan & Gill, 1873), pp. 219–220.

66. [John Roach], *Johnny, I Hardly Knew Ye Irish Comic Songster. Containing all the songs sung by Johnny Roach and the profession in general of the United States* (N.Y.: Frederick A. Brady, 1870).

67. [J. C. Gobrecht], *History of the National Home for Disabled Volunteer Soldiers…at Dayton, Ohio* (Dayton, O.: United Brethren Printing Establishment, 1875), p. 179.

68. Edward Dyson, *In the Roaring Fifties* (New South Wales Bookstall Co., 1906), p 145.

69. James Porter & Herschel Gower, *Jeannie Robertson* (Knoxville: U. of Tennessee Press, 1995), p. 156; Marianne Moore, *Selected Letters*, ed. Bonnie Costello. (New York: Penguin, 1997), p. 287.

70. Michael Mulcahy & Marie Fitzgibbon, *The Voice of the People: Songs and History of Ireland* (Dublin: O'Brien, 1982), p. 175.

71. Lawrence Flick, "The Way to Tipperary is Where the River Shannon Flows," *Kansas City Star* (Jan. 29, 1915), p. 18 [rptd. from the New York *Sun*].

72 *Idaho Daily Statesman* (Boise) (April 11, 1916), p. 9.

73. p. 5 and p. 4 respectively.

74. David Craig & Michael Egan, *Extreme Situations* (London: Macmillan, 1979), p. 73.

75. W. B. Yeats, ed., *A Book of Irish Verse* (London: Methuen, 1895), pp. 238–241; Padraic Colum, ed., *Broadsheet Ballads* (Dublin: Maunsel & Co., 1913), pp. 76–77.

76. *Young Squire Reynolds's Welcome Home to Ireland. To which are added II. Larry's Ghost. III. De Night before Larry was Stretch'd* (Monaghan, Ire.: n.p., 1788).

77. Colum, *Broadsheet*, p. xv.

78. Gregory, Augusta, Lady, *Aristotle's Bellows* (N.Y.: Putnam, 1921), p. 54.

79. Nora A. McGuinness, *The Literary Universe of Jack B. Yeats* (Washington, D.C.: Catholic Universities of America Press, 1991), pp. 206, 217.

80. Oliver St. John Gogarty, *As I Was Going Down Sackville Street* (N.Y.: Harcourt, 1937), pp. 339–340.

81. Oliver St. John Gogarty, *Start from Somewhere Else* (Garden City, N.Y.: Doubleday, 1955), p. 182.

82. Kathleen Hoagland, ed., *1000 Years of Irish Poetry* (N.Y.: Devin-Adair, 1948), pp. 273–274; Susan Mitchell, ed., *Secret Springs of Dublin Song* (Dublin: Talbot Press, 1918), p. 10; "Zoilus" [Robert Y. Tyrrell], "To the Editor," *Kottabos* II (1877), pp. 111–112.

83. W. B. Yeats ed., *The Oxford Book of Modern Verse* (Oxford: Clarendon, 1936), p. xxxv.

84. Louis MacNiece, *Modern Poetry: A Personal Essay* (Oxford: Oxford U. P., 1938), p. 180.

85. Babette Deutsch, *Poetry in Our Time* (N.Y.: Holt, 1952), p. 33; Horace Reynolds, "Dr. Gogarty in Eighteenth-Century Dublin," *New York Times Book Review* (Dec. 7, 1941), p. 6.

86. Dalton Trumbo, *Johnny Got his Gun* (1939; rpt. N.Y.: Bantam Books, 1967), p. v. and front cover.

87. Shaun O'Nolan, *Enniskillen Dragoon/Johnny I Hardly Knew You*. No. 3211. Sound rec. (N.Y.: Columbia Record Co., n.d. [1927]); Dan Sullivan's Shamrock Band, *Johnny, I Hardly Knew Ye* Sound rec. (N.Y.: Victor V-29042, n.d. [1929]).

88. "Johnny, I Hardly Knew Ye," *People's Songs Bulletin* IV (Feb., 1949), p. 3.

89. Patrick Galvin, *Irish Street Songs*. Sound rec. (N.Y.: Riverside 12-613, n.d. [1956]).

90. D. K. Wilgus, "Record Reviews," *Midwest Folklore* VII (1957), p. 250.

91. Cynthia Gooding, *Languages of Love*. Sound rec. (N.Y.: Riverside RLP 12-827, n.d. [1958]); Glenn Yarborough, *Here We Go, Baby*. Sound rec. (N.Y.: Elektra EKL-135, n. d. [1958]).

92. Emma Donoghue, *Hood* (London: Hamish Hamilton, 1995), p. 275.

93. Dominic Behan, *Ireland Sings* (London: Music Sales Ltd., 1973), p. 56. The Clancys and Makem appear to bear responsibility for the idea of a *boneless* "chickenless egg," which is how the line is now usually sung. John Patrick Shanley, *Beggars in the House of Plenty* (N.Y.: Dramatists Play Service, 1992), turns Johnny into a "mindless, boneless" chicken-less egg (p. 37). One fears that the change came via the unconscious influence of "boneless chicken." A more recent, more plausible couplet is reported only once: "You're a hopeless shell of a man on a peg / And you'll have to be put where you're bound to beg" (*Mudcat Discussion Forum*. <http://mudcat.org/thread.cfm?threadid=2570#918970>. Accessed August 1, 2011).

94. Maureen O'Hara, *Her Favorite Irish Songs*. Sound rec. (N.Y.: Columbia CL-1750, n.d. [1962]).

95. Dropkick Murphys, *The Meanest of Times*. Sound rec. (Born & Bred Records, 2007); The Robert Shaw Chorale, *Irish Folk Songs*. Sound rec. (N.Y.: RCA Victor LSCV-2992 [1968]); The West Coast Mennonite Chamber Choir, *And Night Shall End*. Sound rec. (N.p.: Mennonite Central Committee Supportive Care Services IKR014CD, 2003); Joan Baez, *Rare, Live and Classic*. Sound rec. (N.Y.: Vanguard VCD3-125/127, 1993).

96. Janis Ian, *The Best of Janis Ian: The Autobiography Collection*. Sound rec. (Nashville, Tenn.: Rude Girl Records, 2008).

97. Easterhouse, *Contenders*. Sound rec. (N.p.: Cherry Red UK, 2001).

98. Steeleye Span, *Rocket Cottage*. Sound rec. (London: Chrysalis, 1976); Ailish Tynan & Iain Burnside, *A Purse of Gold: Irish Songs by Herbert Hughes*. Sound rec. (N.p.: Signum Classics, 2007); Ann Murray & Graham Johnson, *Irish Songs*. Sound rec. (N.p.: Classical.com Music,

2009); Musical Blades, *Piratically Correct*. Sound rec. (N.p.: Musical Blades, 2008).

99. "Johnny Chad Mitchell Trio"<http://www.youtube.com/watch?v=fQkphdGl-J8>. Accessed August 1, 2011; The Chad Mitchell Trio, *Mighty Day on Campus*. Sound rec. (N.Y.: Kapp KL1262, 1962).

100. E. Bowers & P. B. Isaacs, "Write a Letter to My Mother" (N.Y.: Isaacs, 1864).

101. Harriet N. K. Arnold, ed., *The Poets and Poetry of Minnesota* (Chicago: S. P. Rounds, 1864), pp. 164, 166.

102. Sparling, *Irish Minstrelsy*, pp. 214–215.

103. All of the preceding are from *Mudcat Discussion Forum* <http://mudcat.org/thread.cfm?threadid=2570#918970>. Accessed August 1, 2011.

104. "David Gardiner," *Janis Ian Forum*. May 1, 2010. <http://www.janisian.com/forum/showthread.php?9655Johnny-I-Hardly-Knew-Ye-for-the-chop> Accessed July 30, 2011.

105. Bud Ford & Donna Ford, *The Cripple Creek Dulcimer Book* (Pacific, Mo.: Mel Bay, 1977), unpaginated.

106. Kathy Kelly, *Other Lands Have Dreams* (Oakland, Calif.: Counterpunch/AK Press, 2005), p. 70; Doniger, *Implied Spider*, p. 102.

107. *World Can't Wait. October 2, 2006 Evening at Cooper Union*. <http://video.google.com/videoplay?docid=356865038486 6134030#>. Accessed July 20, 2011.

Joan Wile, *Grandmothers Against the War: Getting Off our Fannies and Standing Up for Peace* (N.Y.: Citadel, 2008), pp. 164–165.

Joan Baez prefaces a 1974 performance by emphasizing the song's relevance to veterans of the Vietnam War (*Joan Baez "Johnny I Hardly Knew Ye,"* 1974 live performance. <http://www.youtube.com/watch?v=UiMt5-V-tQ4>. Accessed August 8, 2011.

The latest twist to the legend at least absolves Gilmore of being a propagandizing opportunist. According to Stephen E. Woodworth, ed., *American Civil War*. 2 vols. (Detroit: Gale/CENGAGE, 2008), p. 134:

"When Johnny Comes Marching Home" is Gilmore's reversal of an Irish antiwar song, "Johnny I Hardly Knew Ye," in which a soldier's wife laments her returning husband's injuries....

Gilmore rewrote the message of the song to comfort his sister Annie, who was engaged to a captain in the Union light artillery named John O'Rourke: "When Johnny comes marching home again. Hurrah! Hurrah!"...

I have found no contemporaneous evidence for this assertion; the immediate source of the story appears to be the Nebraska Historical Society's recommendation that John O'Rourke's house in Plattsmouth, Nebraska, be recognized as a Historic Place by the U.S. National Parks Service (Sec. 8, p. 1):

In 1875 [O'Rourke] returned to Milwaukee, Wisconsin[,] to marry his longtime girlfriend, Annie Maria Gilmore. Gilmore is noted as being the sister of the New York Band Director Patrick Sarsfield Gilmore.

Since Gilmore's song was published in 1863, it would have been an unusually long engagement even for the nineteenth century, when, as E. Anthony Rotundo writes in *American Manhood* (N.Y.: Basic Books, 1993), p. 118, two-year engagements "were common" but one of eight years was extremely unusual.

In the absence of documentation, O'Rourke seems to be associated with the song through family tradition alone.

A native New Yorker, Jonathan Lighter is editor of the *Historical Dictionary of American Slang*, the remaining volumes of which will be published by Oxford University Press. His articles have appeared in *American Speech, War, Literature & the Arts,* and the *Atlantic.* He attributes his interest in folk song to frequent media exposure in childhood to Burl Ives and "The Ballad of Davy Crockett."

Dr. Lighter, Lecturer in English at the University of Tennessee, lives with his wife Jane in Knoxville.

www.ingramcontent.com/pod-product-compliance
Lightning Source LLC
Chambersburg PA
CBHW061155040426
42445CB00013B/1695